# WOODFORD

## A Pictorial History

Aerial view of the River Roding at Woodford Bridge. The ancient Saxon 'lower road', now called the Chigwell Road, runs through the picture. It is crossed by the M11 motorway north of the junction with Snakes Lane, where there is a bridge over the River Roding. However, the original course of the river can be seen below the M11 bridge, as the river was 'moved' when the motorway was built. The bridge now carries the Chigwell Road over an area of grassland. The lower green at Woodford Bridge can be seen at the foot of the picture. The Aston Playing Fields can be seen on the right. They were opened on 14 October 1937, when Wanstead and Woodford were presented with their Borough Charter.

# WOODFORD
## A Pictorial History

**Peter Lawrence
and Georgina Green**

**Phillimore**

1995

Published by
PHILLIMORE & CO. LTD.,
Shopwyke Manor Barn, Chichester, West Sussex

ISBN 1 86077 001 0

Printed and bound in Great Britain by
BIDDLES LTD.
Guildford, Surrey

# List of Illustrations

*Frontispiece:* Aerial view of the River Roding at Woodford Bridge

# Acknowledgements

The authors would like to express their thanks to Bill Liddell, formerly of Birkbeck College, University of London, for his guidance and encouragement during the research which laid the foundation for this book. We would also like to thank Ernest Fulcher, President of the Woodford Historical Society, for showing us that one never stops learning, and for generously passing on his wealth of knowledge.

# Illustration Acknowledgements

We would like to thank the following for supplying photographs to supplement our own collections: Marsden Anderson, 164; Sylvia Ayling, 165; Sharon Eames, 21; Mrs. J. Gill, 123, 126, 155; Mrs. D. Hunt, 104; Wanstead Historical Society, 38; Woodford Golf Club, 145; Woodford Historical Society, 7, 16, 17, 18, 30, 31, 48, 52, 147, 151, 169, 175.

We also gratefully acknowledge the following: Illustrations 5, 6, 13, 42, 45 are reproduced by courtesy of the Essex Record Office; no.15 is reproduced with thanks to Mr. T.H. Prime of Kiplin Hall; no.20 reproduced by courtesy of Phillimore; nos.25, 26 and 27 reproduced by kind permission from *Pedigree of Raikes*, by R.D. Raikes, published in 1980 by Phillimore & Co. Ltd., Chichester, West Sussex; no.34a and b reproduced by courtesy of the William Morris Gallery, Walthamstow; no.55 reproduced by courtesy of London Borough of Redbridge, Libraries Department.

# *Preface*

Many worthy books have been published about Woodford in recent years, so it was with some hestitation that the co-authors agreed to compile *Woodford: A Pictorial History*. The challenge has been to produce a book which is different from those already available, so there is a change of emphasis in this book. Long before the invention of photography many wealthy and powerful families lived in the parish, recognising its convenient proximity to London. The authors have taken this opportunity to use the results of their on-going research into the earlier history of Woodford and are able to include in this book new information along with some little known pictures.

Woodford is fortunate in that nearly all the parish archives have survived since 1600 and are held at the Essex Record Office. This, and the gradual destruction of many fine old houses, led to an interest in local history earlier this century, which culminated in the formation of the Woodford and District Antiquarian Society in 1932. The authors are currently the chairman and secretary of this society (now called Woodford Historical Society) and have been able to call on information and pictures held by the society for the compilation of this book. They owe a particular debt of gratitude to those who have written papers for the society in the past, particularly Mr. E.J. Erith.

The authors would also like to pay tribute to the vast photographic record of Woodford built up by another member of the society, Reg Fowkes, who was also President of the Woodford Photographic Society. His own publication, *Woodford then and now*, cannot be surpassed, and it is for this reason that this book takes a much deeper look at Woodford before the invention of photography. Reg Fowkes passed away on 5 May 1994 and as a family man, local historian and friend he is sadly missed.

This book is dedicated to his memory.

# Introduction

Woodford, which is now part of the London Borough of Redbridge, is situated on the north-east boundary of Greater London. The parish started to be built up when the railway brought a link to London in 1856 but the majority of the housing is 1930s suburbia. However, one or two grand houses remain from the many mansions of the 18th century, and remnants of Epping Forest survive to remind residents of their rural past.

The ancient parish was centred on the Roding valley and was bordered to the east, north and west by forest. The fertile river valley had been cleared for agriculture by our early ancestors and the tree clearance had been extended by the Romans who needed timber for building and food for the vast population of their newly established city of London. The Normans introduced the idea of a legal forest and created the Forest of Essex over a wide area c.1130. Hainault Forest and Epping Forest became recognised as two separate entities much later.

The name Woodford goes back to Saxon times when the early road must have crossed the River Roding by a ford, close to Hainault Forest. The Chapman and André map of 1777 shows tree cover stretching right to Woodford Bridge and it was not until 1851 that an Act was passed for the disafforestation of Hainault Forest. In 1853 over 90 per cent of the forest was grubbed up and the land put under the plough. The Saxon settlement was probably centred on the east side of the River Roding and two village greens survive at Woodford Bridge to this day. By the 13th century a new manor house had been built on the extreme western side of the parish and a church was founded beside the manor house. The earliest mention of this dates from 1177 when it was recorded as belonging to the canons of the Holy Cross of Waltham who owned the manor. This district came to be known as Church End (now South Woodford). Two other hamlets, Woodford Row (now Woodford Green) and Woodford Wells, evolved on the western edge of the parish, along the high ridge close to Epping Forest.

The Saxon road (known as the lower road) was a main route from London via Leytonstone, crossing the Roding at Woodford and then through Chigwell and Abridge northwards to the east of Epping, and on towards Bishops Stortford. It was along this road that the body of St Edmund, king of the Saxons, who died a martyr at the hands of the Danish invaders, was taken to its final resting place at Bury St Edmunds in 1013. The other roads in Woodford at that time were little more than local tracks. Roding Lane North linked Woodford Bridge with roads to Barking Abbey via Ilford. A road along the high ridge led through the forest as a track to Epping. This became known as the High Road when it was extended from Woodford Wells to Epping, via Loughton.

During the medieval period Woodford was largely an agricultural community. But as time went by a number of wealthy citizens of London who wanted a rural retreat not too far from the City were attracted to the parish and built themselves prestigious houses. After the Dissolution of Waltham Abbey in 1540 the manor was granted to a succession of influential gentlemen which increased the desirability of the parish. The strange custom of inheritance by the youngest son (known as Borough English) was traditional in the descent of the principal manor. In 1710 the manor was purchased by Sir Richard Child and was amalgamated with Wanstead manor.

By the middle of the 18th century houses in Woodford were described by a Swedish visitor as 'of brick, several storeys high, well built, and some of them handsome. The inhabitants are partly farmers, but still more gentlemen'. This confirms Daniel Defoe's description of the increase in buildings in the vicinity as mostly larger houses for the richer inhabitants. Many of these were bankers, traders or retired East India captains and ship owners. Woodford must be one of very few parishes where several negro servants have been recorded, although past residents have connections with many foreign lands including France, Holland, Germany, Italy and Turkey as well as the East Indies and America.

At this time the management of local affairs was organised in every parish by the vestry and Woodford was no exception. Fortunately the parish records survive almost complete and give a detailed picture of the running of the parish from Stuart times up to the Victorian era. The parish had four principal officers, elected each year to manage its affairs. The rôles of the Surveyor of Highways, the Parish Constable, and Overseer of the Poor are self-explanatory; the two Churchwardens administered other local matters. They were also responsible for the fabric of the church and the building was extended in 1621 and 1694, a tower was added in 1708 and the church was largely rebuilt in 1816-7. There were many other occasions when lesser repairs were recorded. The parish population was about 70 families in 1676, and 1,745 people were recorded living in 273 houses in 1801. Most of these were either the wealthy families and their servants, shopkeepers and tradesmen, skilled workers like the miller and blacksmith, dressmakers and teachers, or manual workers like the many agricultural labourers. Apart from market gardening and cattle fattening, the principal crop grown in Woodford was hay for the London markets and the many horses kept in the parish. There was very little industry recorded in Woodford.

The Woodford New Road was built in 1829 by the Middlesex & Essex Turnpike Trust and this was extended in the next five years by the Epping & Ongar Highway Trust through the forest of Epping. In 1856 stations were opened at George Lane and Snakes Lane on the new railway line from London to Loughton. This opened up a new way of life, enabling local residents to commute to work in the City each day. Gradually houses were built for the new clerical class. Although most of these were on land taken from the large estates, some were built on 'waste' enclosed from Epping Forest. In the 1860s and '70s Woodford Wood was cleared in the north-west of the parish. In 1878 the Epping Forest Act was passed, safeguarding the remaining forest.

A local board was established in 1873 to take over the responsibilities of the Parish Vestry in running local affairs. The population had more than doubled since 1800, with 4,609 people recorded in the 1871 census. Education was available at the National School in Sunset Avenue and at a similar school attached to St Paul's Church at Woodford Bridge. By this time The Chigwell and Woodford Bridge Gas Company had established a works at the eastern end of Snakes Lane but it was not until 1926 that electricity was available to Woodford homes. The Jubilee Hospital was opened in 1899 and in the next five years Woodford also gained a new post office and a local telephone exchange. A voluntary fire-brigade had also been established by then. The census returns for 1911 record 18,496 people in Woodford.

In 1894 Woodford and Wanstead became urban district councils, 40 years later they amalgamated and in 1937 the Municipal Borough of Wanstead and Woodford was created. With the local government reorganisation in 1965 Woodford and Wanstead joined with Ilford to become the London Borough of Redbridge.

## The Early Communities

Although evidence of prehistoric man has been found in some areas around Woodford, little has been discovered in the parish itself. However it seems likely that our early ancestors settled on the banks of the River Roding, grew crops on the valley floor, fished, and hunted in the forest where they would have gathered what natural food they could find. Similarly, although there was a significant Roman presence in the district, nothing specific has been found in Woodford itself. However the course of Roding Lane North lies along a Roman Road which led from Stratford to Great Dunmow.

As has already been mentioned, Woodford became properly established on the eastern bank of the River Roding in Saxon times. It is probable that the settlement consisted of a number of wooden huts with walls made of branches, twigs and mud, and roofs thatched with reeds from the river-side. Smaller huts would have been erected for specific use, such as cooking, brewing, spinning and weaving, carpentry etc. and there would have been one or two larger huts for habitation. Family groups would have lived together, with alcoves providing a minimum of privacy. The community would have farmed on the open hillside, with a central common where their animals could graze. In the autumn the pigs would have been taken into the forest to fatten them up on acorns and nuts before being killed and salted down to provide meat for the long winter months.

As time went by the most respected member of the community would have become their leader, later to be called the lord of the manor. There are indications that the first manor house may have been on the high point of Roding Lane North, although by the 13th century the lord of the manor lived at the western side of the parish. At the time of Domesday Book in 1086 the manor belonged to the canons of the Holy Cross of Waltham. It shows that, compared with neighbouring manors, Woodford was a relatively prosperous community, perhaps benefiting from the association with the Abbey. No doubt the community suffered with the Black Death, as we know that the priest, William Rous, died a victim of the plague in 1349. By then there were also settlements by the green at Woodford Row and at Woodford Wells.

After the Dissolution of Waltham Abbey in 1540 lords of the manor of Woodford included Sir John Lyon, alderman and grocer, later to become Lord Mayor of London; Sir Anthony Browne, Master of the Horse; Edward Fiennes, Lord Clinton and Say; and Robert Whetstone, citizen and haberdasher of London. The manor stayed in Whetstone's family until 1639 and in 1640 it was acquired by Sir Thomas Rowe, explorer and diplomat. We cannot know how much time any of these gentlemen actually spent in Woodford, but it is recorded that the poet George Herbert spent the year 1628 at the house of his brother, Sir Henry Herbert, in the parish.

The Reformation had other effects on the community. John Larke, who had been the parish priest for a few months in 1526, was executed at Tyburn in 1544 for refusing to acknowledge Henry VIII's supremacy. A later incumbent at Woodford, Henry Sydall, was less strict in his views and managed to sway from Catholicism to Protestantism as the political climate changed. From 1589-1619 the Rector of St Mary's was Robert Wright who was Chaplain to Queen Elizabeth and later James I and held several other prestigious positions so he would seldom have visited Woodford. A curate would have taken services in his place. In 1622 Wright was ordained Bishop of Bristol and a few years later became Bishop of Lichfield and Coventry. The new rector in 1619 was William Isaacson who took a much greater part in Woodford life. It was during his time that the church was enlarged, thanks to the generosity of Elizabeth Elwes who gave a substantial sum so that the north wall of the church could be pulled down and an additional aisle erected in 1621.

Few records have survived about Woodford from before 1600 and it is not easy to find out about individuals or houses which existed in Woodford before that time. By then the parish had begun to expand with wealthy London merchants building country retreats in this rural village. In about 1607 a brick kiln was established near the top of Oak Hill (close to the present *Woodford Moat House Hotel*) and this flourished for nearly 200 years. This, and other local kilns, probably provided the bricks for many of the mansions which were built for these wealthy Londoners.

Up until that time houses would have been constructed with the traditional timber-frame, infilled with wattle and daub. The more prosperous residents would have displayed their wealth by using much more timber than was necessary to support the structure. A few of the larger houses survived into the 19th century, such as Hereford House (*see* illustration 47) and Grove House. Little Monkhams in Monkhams Lane is probably the last remaining timber-framed house to survive in anything like its original state. Although added to a number of times, the construction of the central core seems to indicate origins in the Tudor period. Once bricks became fashionable those who could not afford to rebuild their houses either covered them with plaster, or built a brick façade. However timber construction was still used in cottages for the poorer people.

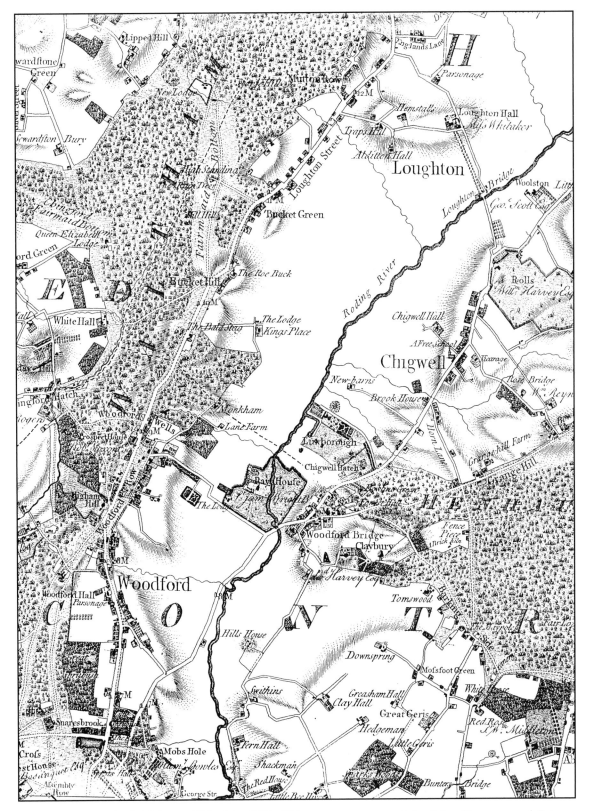

**1** Chapman & André Map published in 1777. This map was surveyed by John Chapman and Peter André, both land surveyors and engravers, in 1772-4 and published in 1777 at a scale of 2½ inches to one mile. It shows clearly the proximity of Hainault Forest to the hamlet at Woodford Bridge, while the mass of Epping Forest is over to the west of the parish. The River Roding lies in the valley between.

**2** The Abbey Church of Waltham Holy Cross and St Lawrence. In 1060 King Harold rebuilt the church at Waltham Abbey and established there a college of secular canons under a dean. It became a priory in 1177 and an abbey 13 years later. Although the abbey was destroyed in 1540, the church survived the Dissolution as it was used as their parish church by the local people. Among the grants made to the canons by King Harold was the manor of Woodford.

**3** Memorial to Rowland Elrington (d.1595). One of the earliest memorials in St Mary's Church, this tells us that Rowland Elrington was a haberdasher and Merchant Adventurer, late of London, who had married Agnes Cage. His will indicates that he owned property which was later part of the Harts estate at Woodford Green, and that there were no surviving children when he died. His brother, William, inherited the Woodford holding and additional estates in Barking, while another brother, Edward, inherited property at Matching and High Laver.

**4** Memorial to Elizabeth Elwes (d.1625).

Elizabeth was the daughter of Robert Gabott (or Gabbott) of Acton Burnell, Salop and on 19 February 1570 she married Geoffrey Elwes at St Mary Bothaw, the London parish where he resided. Her husband rose to prominence within the City, becoming Master of the Merchant Taylors' Company 1604-5, an Alderman of the City in 1605 and Sheriff of London 1607-8. Geoffrey held considerable property in London and Hertfordshire as well as Woodford.

In 1610 Elizabeth had become the sole heir to her brother Henry Gabott of Rainham in Essex who had been a Merchant of London. She and her husband must have suffered great distress at the death of their nephew, Sir Gervase Elwes, who was executed on Tower Hill on 25 November 1615. He had been Lieutenant of the Tower at the time Sir Thomas Overbury was poisoned there and was held responsible for his death. But Elizabeth's greatest blow must have been the death of her husband on 14 May 1616. She was to live nearly ten years more, and it seems probable that most of this time would have been spent in Woodford, before she was laid to rest with her husband at St Mary Bothaw. She died on 11 November 1625 and left £40 to buy land, the rent from which was to be given to the poor of Woodford. Her memorial is on the north wall of St Mary's Church, as it was Elizabeth who funded a new aisle on the north side of the church in 1621.

**5** Sir Thomas Rowe (d.1644).

**6** Entry for Sir Thomas Rowe in the Woodford Burial Register. Sir Thomas Rowe was born at Leyton in about 1580, matriculated as a commoner of Magdalen College, Oxford, in 1593 and soon took up a position in the court of Queen Elizabeth where he became very popular. He was knighted in 1604 when still only 24 years old. In 1609 Henry, Prince of Wales, sent him on the first of three voyages of discovery to the West Indies, during which he sailed 300 miles up the 'River of Amozones', until then unknown to English explorers.

In 1614 James I appointed him Ambassador to the Great Mogul, Emperor of Hindustan, in north-west India. He was instructed to negotiate a commercial treaty for the East India Company and his skills in diplomacy laid the foundations for the expansion of British India. In 1621 Rowe was sent to Constantinople (Istanbul, in Turkey) where he succeeded in mediating a peace treaty between Turkey and Poland with the liberation of many Polish exiles at Constantinople. Rowe also managed to improve relations between England and Algiers, resulting in the release of over 700 English captive mariners. While in Turkey he collected a large number of manuscripts which he eventually gave to the Bodleian Library at Oxford and he also brought back the Alexandrian Mss of the Greek Testament (now in the British Museum) as a present to James I from the patriarch of the Greek church.

In 1629 he was again sent as peace envoy to negotiate a treaty between Sweden and Poland and, having succeeded in this, he finalised a treaty with Denmark on his way home. Rowe won the respect of many foreign leaders, but when he returned to England was given little reward for his effort. For six years he lived in retirement on limited means with his wife, Eleanor, daughter of Sir Thomas Cave, even though Charles I owed him a vast sum for some diamonds which he had purchased for the king at Constantinople. Finally, in 1637, he was appointed Chancellor of the Order of the Garter and granted a pension.

When he was at home, between missions, Sir Thomas Rowe served his countrymen as a Member of Parliament and also wrote several memoirs about his foreign adventures. In 1640 he became a member of the Privy Council and in that year he acquired the manor of Woodford. Sadly, he died four years later and was buried at St Mary's Church, right by the communion table, on 8 November 1644. In his will he left £80 towards the construction of a new aisle 'whensoever the Parish should demand it' and this was eventually built 50 years later at a total cost of £126 5s. Sir Thomas Rowe was learned, devout, reliable and yet charming; devoted to the king, though lightly rewarded in his service. It is known that a Dr. Gerard Langbaine wrote an epitaph to Sir Thomas Rowe but no memorial to him was ever erected.

**7** Grove House (later known as Essex House), *c.*1820. This house was built in 1580 by John Lambert, citizen and grocer of London and of the Merchant Adventurers Company. It stood beside Woodford Green, close to the present site of the Hawkey Hall. In *c.*1617 a room was extensively decorated with wall paintings showing a variety of pastoral scenes. The timber-framed house was demolished in 1832 and a new house was built which incorporated a number of relics from the earlier house. This became known as Essex House. It was destroyed by a flying bomb in 1944.

**8** Little Monkhams in Monkhams Lane is probably the oldest surviving (but much altered) building in Woodford. Although the external timbers were added during a restoration in 1920, it contains part of the timber-framing of an earlier house. It is possible that this is the dwelling mentioned in 1527 when Rauffe Johnson, husbandman of Woodford, leased for 60 years, 'one grove, Monkon Grove, as now enclosed with ditches and hedges, and a sufficient dwelling-house, builded thereon, suitable for a husbandman to dwell in, at 40s. yearly rent'.

**9** Lanehurst, 403 High Road, Woodford Green. Lanehurst, which is set back from the High Road, close to *The Castle*, is a mid-18th century building. Although the front is of stock brick, the rear of the house is of a much more modest appearance as it is weather-boarded over a timber frame.

**10** and **11** (*right and below*) Nos.645-649 Chigwell Road, Woodford Bridge. These 18th-century cottages were in process of restoration when the first photograph was taken in January 1989. This view is from the rear of the building. So much needed to be done that the cottages were ultimately rebuilt, but keeping to their original appearance. They now add to the character of the Woodford Bridge Conservation Area.

**12** Lees pond also known as Brickfield pond. This is one a number of ponds in Epping Forest which were created when clay was dug out to make bricks. This pond is just across from the *Napier Arms* and the whole area to the west of this is riddled with pits and hollows. A licence was granted to John Russell *c.*1607 enabling him to build a cottage and a brick-kiln and to dig clay in this vicinity to make bricks and tiles. This kiln was still flourishing in 1684 and additional workings operated nearby in the period 1768-87.

# *Traders and Travellers, Gentlemen and Bankers*

A census taken in 1676 shows that Woodford was then home for some 70 families and 18 of them lived in large houses with eight or more hearths, a much higher proportion than in neighbouring parishes. At the other extreme were poorer families who built themselves small cottages at the edge of the forest, illegally enclosing the manorial waste. At this time the Forest Laws were quite strictly enforced and it was recorded in 1630 that there were 13 such enclosures in Woodford, and more were noted in 1670. Humble cottages with small gardens and pigstyes tended to be left alone, but those who had grander ideas were given the choice of paying a fine or demolishing the house and returning the land to the forest.

During the early part of the 18th century it became fashionable to 'take the waters' and mineral springs in many locations were exploited, among them the 'wells' at Woodford. It was in 1722 that a Samuel Goldsmith of Woodford Row, Innholder, was granted permission by the Forest authorities to extend the facilities at his dwelling house known by the Sign of the Wells. The earliest tavern recorded in Woodford was the *Horns Inn* in 1657, better known since the 18th century as *The George*. Other inns recorded in the 1700s include the *White Hart* (the inns of that name at South Woodford and at Woodford Bridge were both listed over 200 years ago) and *The Castle*, previously known as *The Ship and Castle* and *The Castle and Two Brewers*.

In 1710 Richard Child, later Earl Tylney, bought the manor of Woodford. His father, Sir Josiah Child, had amassed a vast fortune at the head of the East India Company and this made his descendants not only wealthy, but influential too. The family already owned the Wanstead manor where no expense had been spared in creating a series of lakes, landscaped with avenues of trees. In 1715 Richard Child decided to build a new Wanstead House which was so magnificent that by 1724 the sight-seers had to be restricted to just two days each week. The Woodford manor house, Woodford Hall, was thus surplus to requirements and was sold to Christopher Crowe, British Consul in Italy. He later sold the house to William Hunt, a tobacco merchant and one of several Directors of the Bank of England who resided at Woodford.

By 1690 it had become clear that the volume of trade based in London was such that the establishment of a 'Bank of England' should be considered. One of the leading promoters was Michael Godfrey, a merchant of great substance, who became Deputy Governor when the Bank of England was established in 1694. The Bank's charter laid down that, apart from the Governor and Deputy Governor, there should be 24 Directors who must each hold £2,000 of stock. All were to be elected annually and later Woodford residents to serve the Bank of England include Michael Godfrey's brother Peter Godfrey of The Rookery, Richard Salway of Salway Lodge, both of whom were Directors, and Job Mathew who was a Governor.

The wealth of Woodford came not only from those who traded wisely in the City—other residents only came to live in the parish after years abroad, earning their fortunes as ship's captains or as agents in far-flung places. Drigue Olmius was the son of a great Hamburg merchant, David Bosanquet lived for many years in Turkey, while Jeffrey Jackson, Robert Preston and Charles Foulis all served as captains with the East India Company during the 18th century. Another gentleman who had travelled abroad was Sir James Wright, British minister in Venice. He brought ideas about making artificial slate back from Italy and set up a small factory on his Ray House estate by the Roding.

As time went by the construction of large houses for the wealthy accelerated and one or two such houses still survive. Hurst House, a stuccoed Queen Anne-style building in Broomhill Walk (near the Churchill statue) is said to have been built in *c*.1714 for Henry Raine, a brewer from Wapping. Thomas North, who was probably another wealthy brewer, this time from Southwark, also built himself a house at Woodford. He and his wife Mary were responsible for the felling of much of Monkham Grove during the period 1737-52. Their house was situated close to the present-day junction of Monkhams Lane and The Green and was called Monkhams. The house was demolished *c*.1820 when the name was transferred to another house which had been built by Sir John Hall in the early 1800s, where Park Avenue is today. The new owner, Brice Pearse, added greatly to his land holding in the early years of the 19th century and, with his neighbour William Mellish of Harts, persuaded the parish to alter the course of Snakes Lane, moving it further south to its present location, so that it did not cut through his vast estate.

In 1767 William Hunt died and his nephew, William Hunt Mickelfield, inherited Woodford Hall. He rebuilt the house in 1771 to a design by Thomas Leverton. The neighbouring Walthamstow manor house, Highams, had been built facing Woodford Green three years earlier and the styles were similar. Woodford Hall was leased to John Goddard, a Rotterdam merchant, in 1777 and in 1801 it was purchased by John Maitland. He wasted no time in inviting Humphry Repton, the leading landscape gardener of his time, to design a new look for the Woodford estate. Repton had already been called in to work for James Hatch at Claybury in 1791 and for John Harman at Highams in 1793.

The lordship of the principal Woodford manor had stayed in the family of Sir Richard Child, passing to his grandson Sir James Tylney-Long who died in 1794 leaving a very young son as his heir. Sadly he died in 1805, so the vast Wanstead and Woodford estates were held in trust for his sister, Catherine Tylney-Long (1789-1825). This young heiress was courted by gentlemen of every rank, but in 1812 she married William Pole-Wellesley, nephew of the Duke of Wellington. This proved to be a most unfortunate choice as in 10 years he squandered her vast fortune and his extravagance was such that the entire contents of Wanstead House had to be auctioned off. This included paintings by Rubens, Titian, and Rembrandt, furniture which had belonged to the Buonaparte family, tapestries, books—so much that it took over a month to complete the sale. Even that did not pay off the debts, so Wanstead House was totally demolished and the fabric sold off as building materials. However, lordship of both the manors of Wanstead and Woodford stayed with Wellesley.

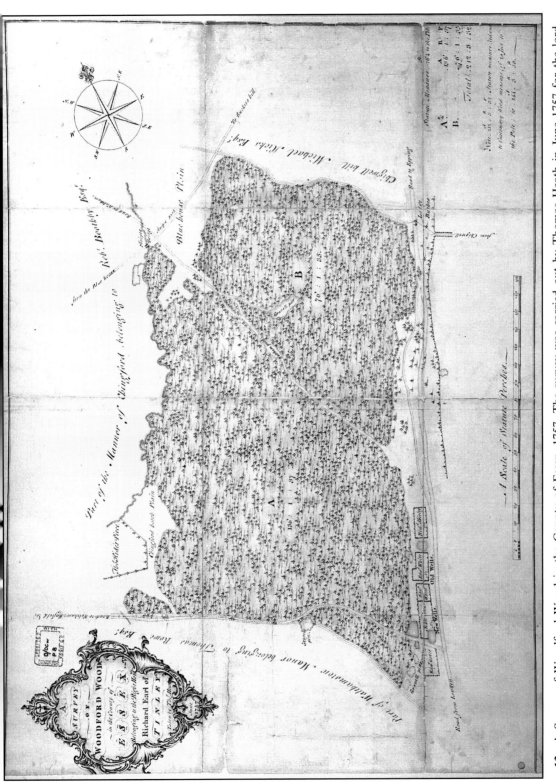

**13** A Survey of Woodford Wood in the County of Essex, 1757. The survey was carried out by Thomas Heath in June 1757 for the lord of the manor, the Right Hon. Richard, Earl of Tinley and shows clearly the location of the 'wells'. Both were close to the High Road—the 'New Wells' were just to the north of the present-day junction with Sydney Road while the 'Old Wells' were south of the junction with Mornington Road.

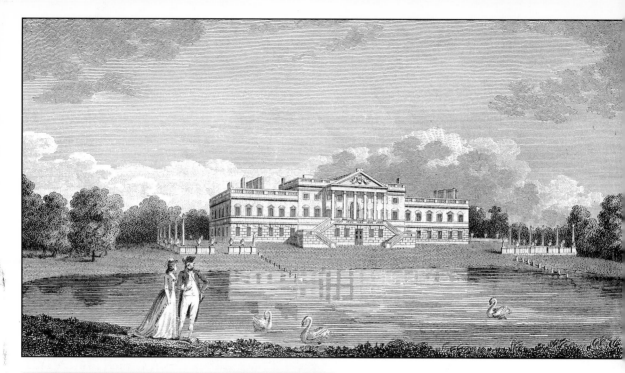

**14** Wanstead House, 1787. The mansion built by Sir Richard Child (lord of the manors of Woodford and Wanstead) in 1715-20 was one of the finest examples of English Palladian architecture. Designed by Colen Campbell, it was 260 feet in length, 75 feet wide and its main front was embellished with a portico supported by six Corinthian columns, reached by a double flight of steps. The spendour of the mansion made Wanstead a fashionable centre and lavish entertainment was arranged for the many guests invited to stay there.

**15** Christopher Crowe (1681-1749). He was born in Northumberland but came to Woodford in *c*.1710 when he purchased Woodford Hall from Sir Richard Child. He was appointed British Consul at Leghorn (Livorno on the west coast of Italy, near Florence) liaising with various Italian dukes as well as keeping in contact with The Hague and Vienna. This gave him ample opportunity to expand both his knowledge of fine art, his contacts in high places, and his personal fortune.

He married Charlotte Lee, Lady Baltimore, a granddaughter of King Charles II and Barbara Villiers. After her death in 1720 Crowe purchased the Baltimore family estate at Kiplin, Yorkshire, from his stepson. Some of his furniture and pictures can be seen at Kiplin Hall, which is owned by charitable trust and open to the public during the summer.

**16** Hurst House, 1 Broomhill Walk, Woodford Green, built in *c*.1714 (at the same time as Wanstead House), is one of the few buildings in Redbridge listed as Grade II*. The line drawing shows the back of the house towards the end of the 18th century when it was used as a school. The original central block (approximately 48 feet) has been extended by the wings at each side.

**17** The photograph of the front of Hurst House was taken *c*.1934. Sadly the house was gutted by fire a couple of years later and the building we see today is largely a reconstruction. The fine staircase and the richly carved architrave of the front door are original and the pilasters and the stone vases on the parapet also survived the fire.

**18** The Godfrey Memorial in St Mary's churchyard photographed soon after its restoration in the mid-1950s. Michael Godfrey (1659-95), a London Mercer, was the first Deputy Governor of the Bank of England when it was founded in 1694. He died a bachelor at the age of 36 while on a mission to the battlefields of Flanders on behalf of the newly established Bank. He owned The Rookery, built by his parents in George Lane, and this passed to Peter Godfrey (1662-1724), Michael's only surviving brother. He was also a prosperous City merchant, a Director of the Bank of England, and of the East India Company, and he served two terms as a Member of Parliament for the City.

The tall Corinthian column of Siena marble was erected over the Godfrey family vault after their descendants had moved away. It was designed by Sir Robert Taylor and is listed as Grade II*.

**19** The Rookery, *c.*1806. It was built, probably around 1675, by Michael Godfrey (1625-89) and served as the family base for nearly a hundred years. For a short time it was the home of William Raikes and after his death the property was registered jointly with two of his sons and George Smith, a banker. It was at this time that the illustration reproduced here was drawn, almost certainly by Humphry Repton. In 1810 John Hanson (1758-1839) purchased the house, moving his large family from Colchester to be nearer the social life of London. He had been High Sheriff of Essex in 1795. It was probably Hanson who pulled down the old house and built a new one a little further down George Lane. Peter Cloves was the next resident at The Rookery and then in the time of William Malins much of the land was taken when the railway was built through the estate, in 1856.

**20** David Bosanquet (1699-1741). Son of a Huguenot refugee, David Bosanquet spent his working life building up the business established by his father as an importer of eastern merchandise such as silks, carpets, spices and leather goods. He lived in Aleppo, Turkey, for a number of years and the painting shows him in local costume. Later he lived in Woodford, although quite where is not known.

**21** Richard Warner (1713-75). Richard Warner was educated at Oxford and qualified as a lawyer but had sufficient money for his needs and he lived the life of a gentleman at Harts. His library amounted to 4,000 books and he was an expert on the works of Plautus and Shakespeare. Richard Warner was a keen botanist and established a fine garden at Harts where he was the first person to grow a gardenia after its introduction into this country. He also published a small volume, *Plantae Woodfordienses*, which lists all the plants growing in the Woodford area in 1771.

**22** Harts House, 1789. The site takes its name from Richard Hert who lived there in 1270, and the illustration is of a house built in 1617 by Sir Humphrey Handforth. He was one of the courtiers of James I and apparently the king frequently visited Harts when he was hunting in the forest nearby. The recently widowed Mrs. John Warner purchased the house in 1722 and after the death of her son, Richard Warner, it passed to his brother's descendants, the Clarke Jervoise family.

**23** Memorial to Charles Foulis (*c*.1714-83). Charles Foulis rose through the ranks in East India Company ships, taking full advantage of the company's rule which allowed captains to trade privately whilst on official voyages. He would take out essential materials, such as sheet lead or copper and return with luxury goods, gems and gold. On his last voyage as an East India captain in 1755, he was allowed to import, duty free, 251 ounces of gold and he went on to own 12 ships. Also he bought and sold East India stock, sometimes dealing with his own captains. Charles Foulis is recorded as resident on the Harts estate at the end of his life and this is where Captain Robert Preston is shown as living a decade later.

The fine memorial in St Mary's Church was placed there as a testimony of gratitude by Robert Preston. It was by John Bacon (1740-99) who had trained in the Wedgwood Company and went on to become much sought after for portrait busts and sepulchral monuments. His son was the architect of the church when it was rebuilt in 1816.

**24** The Slate Factory at Ray House. Sir James Wright (d.1804) served as British minister in Venice before taking up residence at Ray House in Snakes Lane. He established a factory making 'artificial slate' on the estate, using techniques he had seen in Italy for manufacturing clay-based products. The business prospered for some time, with considerable quantities of slate being exported to the West Indies. It had closed by 1811, after about 35 years in business.

**5** William Raikes (1738-1800). William Raikes was born in 1738, son of Robert Raikes, a prosperous printer in Gloucester. His brother, also Robert Raikes (1736-1811), continued the family printing business and achieved fame as the promoter of Sunday Schools in the 1780s. William became a merchant in London, a Director of the South Sea Company and one of the Commercial Commissioners under the Income Act for the City. Family archives describe William Raikes as 'of Valentines' and it would seem that he was the tenant of the Ilford mansion after Sir Charles Raymond, but he was registered as the owner of The Rookery in George Lane by 11 November 1795.

The Raikes memorial in St Mary's churchyard also commemorates Martha Pelly Raikes who died on 14 March 1797. She was the daughter of Job Mathew of West Ham and had married William Raikes at West Ham on 21 October 1762. According to the inscription on the mausoleum, she was a kind and understanding lady; indeed, they were a very amiable couple. William Raikes died on 14 October 1800. Also buried with them is Martha's brother, Job Mathew (1741-1802), a Governor of the Bank of England, and his wife Mary.

**26**  Job Matthew Raikes (1767-1833).

**27**  Charlotte Susanna Raikes (*c.*1779-1821).

William and Mary's third son, Job Matthew Raikes (1767-1833), married Charlotte Susanna Bayly, daughter of Nathaniel Bayly of Jamaica, at St Mary's Church on 30 June 1798. He was a merchant of Alderman's Walk, Bishopsgate, but he died in Marseilles in 1833. His wife had died in 1821 and they were both interred at St Mary's. Their son, Charles Raikes (1812-1885), was in the Bengal Civil Service for 30 years and became a notable writer on India.

**28** The Raikes Memorial (background) and the Hunt Mickelfield Memorial (foreground) in St Mary's churchyard. William Hunt was a tobacco merchant and a Director of the Bank of England who purchased Woodford Hall from Christopher Crowe in 1727. When he died in 1767 the house was inherited by his nephew William Hunt Mickelfield, who was captain of the East India ship *Rochford*. He demolished the old Woodford Hall and had it rebuilt in 1771.

**29**   Grove Hall, 1901.                          **30**   The wrought-iron gates of Grove Hall, *c*.1901.

Grove Hall was built in the early 1700s on a site opposite the top of George Lane, adjacent to a part of the forest known as Woodford Grove. It was built for Sir Peter Eaton whose daughter, Mary, married her cousin, Captain Nicholas Eaton. Their joint family arms decorated the wrought-iron gates. When their son, another Peter Eaton, died a bachelor in 1769 the estate passed to his cousin, Rev. Richard Monins. As he lived in Kent the house was let out and it seems likely that it was the home of Job Mathew, Governor of the Bank of England. In 1854 Grove Hall was bought by Mr. Washington Single who converted it into two dwellings. It was eventually demolished in 1958-9 and an insurance office was built on the site.

**31**   Elmhurst, *c*.1900. This house was originally known as Grove House after the owner, Sylvanus Grove. He came to Woodford in 1770 and had the house built the following year, to a design by Joel Johnson of Walthamstow. The house was later the home of Smith Harrison, a Quaker tea merchant, and his wife Jane, a sister of Lord Lister.

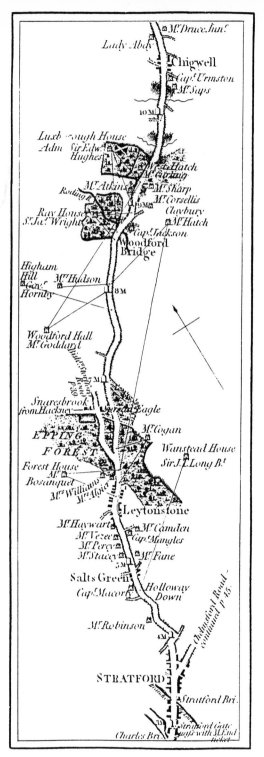

**32** Cary Maps of 1790. John Cary (*c*.1754-1835) was a fine engraver and the quality of his maps made them valuable both to the public and the Post Office. His objective was to feature every 'gentleman's seat' and the lines indicate sight-lines from the highway for those houses off the main routes. The two maps shown are from his 'Survey of the High Roads from London' and are of interest in that they show a number of local residents. See particularly: Mr. Godfrey and Mr. Grove (The Rookery and Elmhurst) at the top of George Lane, Mr. Mathew opposite, Mr. Goddard at Woodford Hall, Mr. Dod (the local physician), Governor Hornby at Higham Hill, Sir James Wright at Ray House, Captain Jackson at Woodford Bridge, Mr. Hatch at Claybury and Mr. Corsellis (at Gwynne House).

**33** Woodford Hall from the Red Book by Humphry Repton, 1801. (Top shows Repton's sketch of 'before' and below how he thought the same scene would look if his suggestions were carried out.) John Maitland bought Woodford Hall from William Hunt Mickelfield in 1801 and wasted no time in asking Humphry Repton to suggest improvements to the estate. Repton felt the chief intrusions were the proximity of the highway and the church to the Hall and he could do little about this other than to re-route the approach road so that they were less obvious. Other proposals included the removal of the kitchen garden and outbuildings which were close to the house, opening up the vista across the estate.

John Maitland allowed the lease granted to John Goddard to run until after the death of his wife, but he had taken up residence at Woodford Hall by 1820. Maitland inherited the manor of Loughton in 1825 and so Woodford Hall was later leased out again.

**34a** William Morris (1797-1847). William Morris (father of the famous designer) married Emma Shelton in 1826 and these miniature portraits were probably painted at the time of their engagement. William was a bill and discount broker in the City and in 1840 the family moved into Woodford Hall. William Morris Jnr. was then aged six and he later recalled his early days 'in the kitchen-garden at Woodford where large blue plums grew on the wall beyond the sweet-herb patch'. The family left Woodford Hall and moved to the Water House in Walthamstow (now the William Morris Gallery) after the death of William Morris Snr., in 1847.

**34b** Emma Shelton (1805-94).

**35**  Claybury Hall, 1806. Claybury is actually in the parish of Ilford, which in 1806 was still part of the parish of Barking, but, like Highams, it is right on the border with Woodford. James Hatch of Bromley, a wealthy malt-distiller, bought the manor in 1786 and soon had the house rebuilt. He also acquired the manors of Chigwell, Luxborough and Monkhams, and Great Gales Farm at Woodford Bridge. Hatch took a keen interest in farming techniques and corresponded with Arthur Young who was writing his *General View of Agriculture in Essex*. In 1889 the estate was sold to the London County Council which built the hospital there, while retaining Claybury Hall within the complex.

**36** Higham Hills (Highams), 1800. The house shown was built in 1768 as the manor house of the Higham Bensted manor and, strictly speaking, it is in Walthamstow. From 1785-90 it was owned by William Hornby, Governor of Bombay, and he sold it to John Harman, a banker. In 1849 Edward Warner bought the manor and Higham House. The Warner family still has strong connections with Walthamstow and the house is now part of Woodford County High School.

**37** Gwynne House at Woodford Bridge. The name of the house comes from 'Guines', a medieval tenement which occupied this site. In 1793 Gwynne House was described as 'a pretty villa built by Caesar Corsellis Esq'. The Corsellis family were Flemings and the name 'Caesar' indicates the connection by marriage with Sir Caesar Child, who lived at Claybury in the first half of the 18th century. In 1772 Nicholas Caesar Corsellis married Mary Hunt, sister of William Hunt of Woodford Hall. Towards the end of the century Gwynne House was purchased by Henry Burmester, a rich London merchant who took an active part in church affairs. He rebuilt the house in 1816 and much later, in 1909, the house and estate were bought for the Dr. Barnardo's Homes to build their Garden City (*see* illustration 156). Gwynne House is known today as *The Prince Regent Hotel*.

**38** Catherine Tylney-Long (1789-1825). Catherine Tylney-Long inherited the vast wealth of the manor of Wanstead (and the manor of Woodford) at the tender age of five, but it was held in trust until she came of age, by which time her hand in marriage was being sought by numerous suitors, from royalty downwards. On 14 March 1812 she married William Pole-Wellesley, nephew of the Duke of Wellington. Her bridal attire cost well over 1,000 guineas and her necklace was valued at 25,000 guineas, but the groom had not bothered to purchase a ring for his bride! This bad start did not improve and in the next 10 years his gambling and other extravagances led to their financial ruin.

**39** Wanstead House, 1818. The contents of Wanstead House were auctioned off in an attempt to cover Wellesley's debts. The estate was safeguarded by the marriage settlement but the mansion was sold for demolition and nothing remains except the large depression where the house once stood—now a hazard on Wanstead Golf Course.

Catherine died soon after in 1825, and was buried in the family vault at Draycot in Wiltshire. Her husband became the Earl of Mornington and, although financially disgraced, he continued as lord of the manors of Wanstead and Woodford until his death in 1857.

**40** Sir John Hall (1779-1861). John Hall was born in 1779 at Stannington in Yorkshire, and in 1811 he purchased an estate by Snakes Lane and built a house there. It seems that this was the mansion later acquired by Brice Pearse and re-named Monkhams when his older property was demolished. John Hall, J.P., was High Sheriff for Essex in 1817, and Lord Lieutenant of the county. His business interests were ship and insurance broking and he served the country during the Napoleonic Wars by regulating convoys in the English Channel. In 1816 he was appointed Consul-General for Hanover in the United Kingdom and from 1825 to 1853 he was the Hon. Secretary and Treasurer of the Society of Merchants trading with the Continent. He founded the St Katherine's Dock Co. and was knighted in 1831 by William IV. For several years Sir John Hall, K.C.H. was confidential financial adviser to Queen Victoria before he died in Kensington on 21 January 1861 after a long and active life.

**41** William Mellish (1774-1834). William Mellish was the son of Peter Mellish, a prosperous farmer and land owner who became very wealthy when the West India Docks were built, partly on his land. His son was a shipowner and took the opportunity to build a large wharf close by one of the dock entrances. William Mellish built up his own fortune by acquiring government contracts for provisioning the navy during the period of war. He was elected a Subscriber to Lloyd's in 1802, and served as M.P. for Grimsby 1796-1806 and for Middlesex 1806-20. He was also a Director of the Bank of England. William Mellish bought the Harts estate in 1815. He soon demolished the house which had been home to Richard Warner, and built a new, spacious house on the site. In 1832 one of his captains attempted to assassinate him. He died 18 months later, leaving property to the value of nearly three million pounds.

## Parish Life

While the wealthy brought prestige to Woodford, the local people continued village life just as their fathers and grandfathers had done. Sir James Wright's slate factory was virtually the only local industry, although in the 1820s a small optical works was operating just over the northern parish boundary, opposite the *Bald Faced Stag*. Most people were farm labourers or worked in the grand houses with jobs ranging from laundress to ladies' maid or stable lad to butler, depending on training, experience and family connections. Others served the whole community, such as the Radley and Priest families who were blacksmiths, the Meads who were boot and shoe makers and the Noble family who were carpenters and builders.

Village life was under the guidance of the local vestry which met every month to consider the welfare of the poor, health, law and order, and road maintenance as well as matters concerning the church itself. Looking after the poor, the sick and the elderly was an ever-present problem. In the 17th century, money was given to pensioners for clothing and fuel, and later a small almshouse was established at Woodford Bridge. By 1724 the cost of looking after the less fortunate had risen so much that a building was leased from Christopher Crowe for use as a workhouse. Outdoor relief was paid to some, such as widows with young children, or men who had become sick or physically disabled and had families to support. Keeping families in their cottages was cheaper than splitting them up and sending them to different workhouses outside the parish. Orphans were cared for until old enough to serve an apprenticeship and by 1800 it seems that some were sent far away, to the mills in Nottinghamshire or even to work for the Hudson Bay Company in Canada. By this time an old timber-framed building at the top of Monkhams Lane was used as the workhouse and a pesthouse (or isolation hospital) had been built away from the community at the site now used by Bancroft's School. A new workhouse was also built there in 1820 at a cost of £1,000.

The principal officers of the Vestry, the Overseer of the Poor, the Surveyor of Highways, the Parish Constable, and one Churchwarden, were elected each year by the community from among its members and verified by local Justices. The other church-warden was chosen by the Rector and had different responsibilities. Rates were levied on local residents to pay for the various services provided and the rate valuation books give a good indication of the social composition of the community. For example, in 1797/8 John Goddard's Woodford Hall was valued at £180 per year plus £131 for his farm and lands, James Hatch (Gales Farm) at £135, Robert Preston (Harts) at £80, Richard Noble (carpenter and undertaker) at £24, Thomas Rounding (landlord of *The Horse and Well*) at £12, while the properties of poorer residents were valued at between £1 and £12 per year.

Law and order was the responsibility of the Parish Constable and by 1788 the parish had been divided into two districts with separate officers for 'The Town' and for Woodford Bridge. The Parish Constable had to check the accuracy of weights and measures and that ale was of the correct strength. As early as 1694 it is recorded that 'all fellons and vagrants shall be secured and lodged in the Cage and that a strong lock with two keys be provided for it'. The cage was situated opposite the *White Hart*, South Woodford. One key was to be held at the inn and the other with the Constable. The following year we read that Madam Anne Godfrey had given silver plate to the church in memory of her son, Michael Godfrey, to replace that which had been stolen. However, quarter sessions records indicate that crime was not as rife in Woodford as in many Essex villages. By 1826 the parish benefited from the presence of a horse patrol and in 1839 Woodford was brought under the jurisdiction of the Metropolitan police.

When he died in 1644 Sir Thomas Rowe bequeathed £80 to enlarge the church when this became necessary, and the work was eventually carried out in 1694. In 1708 a new tower was built and this is the oldest part of the church still standing today. Throughout the 18th century there were minor repairs to the church, new pews were added, and a gallery was built, but by the early 1800s it had become necessary once again to enlarge the church. John Maitland, living next door to the church at Woodford Hall, was not at all keen on the idea but eventually his objections were overruled and both Maitland and his daughter Isabella gave money for the project. A fund-raising committee was set up, William Pole-Wellesley, lord of the manor, was paid £5 for additional land to extend the churchyard, Charles Bacon was chosen as architect and in 1816 work started on rebuilding the church. The congregation worshipped at St Mary's Church, Wanstead, while the work was in progress. The parish records include a plan showing the allocation of pews in the new church, and this gives a wonderful insight into the local hierarchy.

**2** Manorial Map of Woodford Hall 1700. Although a rather crude map, this shows the church before the tower was built in 1708—notice the lych-gate. The building to the north is Woodford Hall which was then the manor house. It was later the home of Christopher Crowe. Note also the windmills to the north (Lady Thorowgood's Mill) and the west (the Walthamstow Mill) and the houses along the High Road.

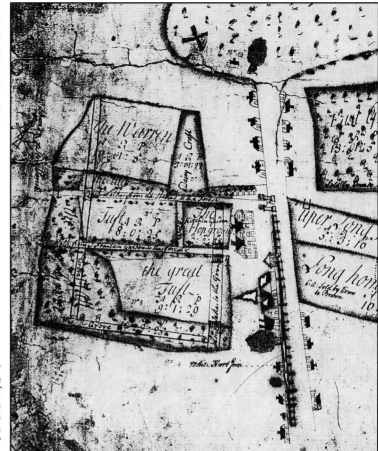

**3** St Mary's Church, 1809. An early picture of the church showing it before the rebuilding in 1816. Note the quantity of trees behind the church. The tomb shown surrounded by railings is that to William Hunt. The columns and the draped urn disappeared at the turn of the century (*see* illustration 28).

# WOODFORD.

The parish-church is a brick building, dedicated to St. Margaret; it consists of a chancel and nave, with north and south ailes; the east end is of considerable antiquity, as appears by the long narrow windows, and niches, which probably had figures in them; *(see the view above;)* the tower is also of brick, with a ring of five bells.

**44**  St Mary's Church, 1814, from Ogborne. Elizabeth Ogborne's *History of Essex* was published in 1814 and the illustrations were 'taken on the spot' by her husband, John Ogborne, an artist and engraver from Chelmsford.

  The church has been dedicated to St Mary since at least the 14th century although there are occasional references to it as St Margaret's, as here. It is likely that the dedication to St Margaret was originally a mistake, repeated in several later publications.

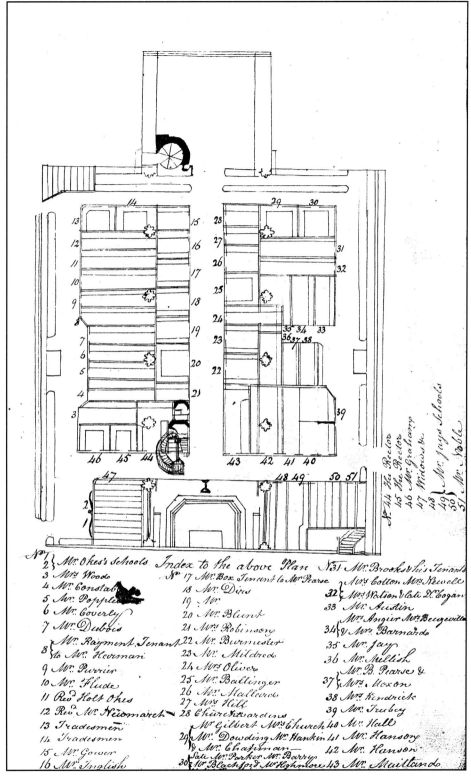

**45** Plan of the allocation of pews in St Mary's Church, 1817. This plan appears in the Vestry Minute Book for July 1817 and shows the seating arrangements proposed for the church once the building work had been completed. The three-tier pulpit can be seen in front of the Rector's pew (44), while the most influential members of the congregation are facing the pulpit: Mr. Maitland of Woodford Hall (43), Mr. Hanson of The Rookery needing two pews for his large family (41-2), Mr. Hall (later Sir John Hall) (40), with Mr. Mellish and Mr. Pearse (36 and 37).

*Woodford Church, Essex. Consecrated July 12. 1817.*

**46**  St Mary's Church, *c.*1850. This was the parish church as Woodford was ending its time as a rural community. By 1851 a large room was being rented at Woodford Bridge so that services could be held there, saving local residents the long walk via the Lower Road and up the hill, through the fields (Churchfields) to St Mary's. St Paul's Church was built at Woodford Bridge in 1854, and All Saints' at Woodford Wells 20 years later.

**47**  Hereford House, Woodford Wells. This building stood at the top of the old Snakes Lane (near the top of Monkhams Lane) and local tradition says it was built as a hunting lodge by the Earl of Essex, Robert Devereux. In 1739 it is said that Price Devereux, 10th Viscount Hereford, lived there and gave the house its name. In 1792 the building was rented out by Mr. Moxon to the Vestry for use as a workhouse, although considerable repairs were needed.

To the Churchwardens and Overseers of the Poor of the
Parish of *Walthamstow* in the *County*
of *Essex* ——————— and the Churchwardens
and Overseers of the Poor of the Parish of *Woodford*
in the *County* —— of *Essex*

*Essex*
to wit. } **Whereas** Complaint hath been made unto Us, whose Names are
hereunto set, and Seals affixed, being Two of His Majesty's
Justices of the Peace in and for the *County* of *Essex*
aforesaid, (One whereof being of the Quorum) by the Churchwardens and
Overseers of the Poor of the said Parish of *Walthamstow*
That *Mary Lindsay Singlewoman* ————

ha*th* come to inhabit in the said Parish of *Walthamstow*
not having gained a legal Settlement there, nor having produced any
Certificate acknowledging *her* to be settled elsewhere, and
now actually become chargeable to the same; WE, the said Justices, upon
due Proof made thereof, as well upon the Examination of the said

*Mary Lindsay*

upon Oath, as other Circumstances, do adjudge the same to be true, and do
also adjudge the Place of the legal Settlement of the said *Mary*

*Lindsay* ————

to be in the Parish of ~~that~~ *Woodford*
in the *County* of *Essex*

THESE are therefore in His Majesty's Name to require you, the
said Churchwardens and Overseers of the Poor of the said Parish of
*Walthamstow* or some or one of you, or any proper Person
or Persons to be employed by you, to remove and convey the said

*Mary Lindsay* ————

from and out of your said Parish of *Walthamstow*
to the said Parish of *Woodford* and *her*
deliver unto the Churchwardens and Overseers of the Poor there, or to
some or one of them, together with this our Order, or a true Copy thereof,
who are hereby required to receive and provide for *her*
according to Law.

GIVEN under our Hands and Seals, the *sixteenth* Day of
*September* in the Year of our Lord One Thousand Eight
Hundred and Twenty-*six*

**48** Certificate of Settlement for Mary Lindsay, 1826. Mary Lindsay, unmarried and unable to support herself financially, had appealed to the Walthamstow Vestry for help. As she had not been born in that parish, nor been resident there long term, they had applied to the local Justice to determine which parish was responsible for her welfare. This certificate authorises them to take her to Woodford, and it is her proof that the Woodford Vestry should provide for her.

**49** Walthamstow Mill, *c.*1781. The map drawn *c.*1700 (*see* illustration 42) shows two windmills. Lady Thorowgood's Mill, or the Woodford Hall manor mill did not continue in use long after the manor was sold in 1710. Land for the Walthamstow Mill was granted in 1676, on a site just opposite the *Napier Arms* (hence Mill Plain), and, although the picture above shows it to be in poor repair, the mill continued to operate until it blew down in 1800. An earlier mill at Woodford Green (near *The Castle*) is shown on the map dated *c.*1641, shown as illustration 73.

**50** The Old Mill, 1877. Domesday Book records the existence of a watermill in 1066 but this had gone twenty years later. A farmhouse is recorded close to a watermill in 1609 and this later became a beerhouse known as the *Old Mill*. It developed a somewhat dubious reputation and ceased business before the First World War. The premises were later used for The Mill Garage and demolished when the M11 motorway was built and the Charlie Brown roundabout enlarged.

*The Old Mill Inn.*

**51** Memorial to John Popplewell (*c*.1757-1829). John Popplewell was a surgeon who spent his life looking after his neighbours. He lived at Holmleigh, opposite the church (now part of Gates of Woodford), and took a keen interest in church affairs. John and his sisters Ann and Rebecca were generous benefactors to the community which regarded them with respect and affection. A similar tribute to that at St Mary's Church (shown above) was placed in St Peter and St Paul's Church at Chingford.

# Travel and Transport

Along the Woodford road there comes a noise
Of wheels, and Mr. Rounding's neat postchaise
Struggles along, drawn by a pair of bays,
With Rev. Mr. Crow and six small Boys;
Who ever and anon declare their joys,
With trumping horns and juvenile huzzas,
At going home to spend their Christmas days,
And changing Learning's pains for Pleasure's toys.

Thomas Hood lived at the Lake House in Wanstead from 1832-5. His charming sonnet, written in 1832, reminds us of the sounds and way of travel that were familiar to our ancestors, but it fails to project how bad the roads could be—deep-rutted mud in winter and white with dust in the summer.

Woodford's residential nature was emphasised by its roads, as by the early 18th century it was comparatively easy to reach London, but more difficult to travel out into Essex. Of the two present main roads from London, the 'Lower Road', now called the Chigwell Road, was subject to flooding by the River Roding and by the mill stream. Even in recent years flooding has caused problems but the building of the M11 motorway and the North Circular Road interchange meant a new channel for the river and flood alleviation measures have been introduced. For centuries there were problems at the Woodford Bridge river crossing until in 1771 the wooden bridge was replaced at the second attempt by a brick and stone bridge. In 1785 responsibility for its upkeep passed to the Middlesex and Essex Turnpike Trust. This bridge served travellers continuously until its replacement in 1962. However, during the building of the M11 in the 1970s the course of the river was moved closer to the junction with Snakes Lane, making the ancient crossing site redundant (*see* Frontispiece).

In contrast to the 'Lower Road', the 'Upper Road' or High Road has only been a main road since the 17th century. In 1721 the Middlesex and Essex Turnpike Trust developed the road as far as Woodford Wells. In 1829 the trust built the Woodford New Road and in 1834 the Epping and Ongar Highway Trust cut the Epping New Road through the forest to Epping. Both new roads were bypasses to cut out built-up areas and steep inclines. Until the 20th century there were only two roads in Woodford that connected the upper and lower roads—Snakes Lane and George Lane.

Stage coaches passing through Woodford on the Norwich run would stop at either *The George*, *White Hart* (High Road) or *The Castle*, depending on the carrier. In 1788 the total journey time from London to Norwich via Woodford and Newmarket was just under 15 hours. There were also 'short stage' coaches for commuters into London; many of them sported highly coloured livery. For example Mr. May of Woodford stuck silver stars all over his coach to attract customers on his Chigwell to London run.

Through the centuries local roads would have echoed to the sounds of animals being shepherded to the London markets, heavy carts moving slowly along the roads from dawn until dusk, and the clatter of many horsemen. When Peter Kalm, a Swedish botanist, visited Richard Warner at Harts on 28 February 1748, he described the roads as 'full of travellers, on foot and on horseback, in wagons and carts, who travel backwards and forwards, so that one often has, as it were, to steer through them'.

One of the innovations brought about by the Industrial Revolution was the railway, and a line was built from London to Romford by the Eastern Counties railway in 1839. A branch line from Stratford to Loughton was opened in 1856, with stations at George Lane and Snakes Lane where there were level crossing gates across the roads. Not only did the railway cut the parish in two, it started the break-up of some of the large estates. Once it became possible to travel to London to work, it became economically viable to start building 'villas' for the clerical workers who could afford to commute each day. This was the start of the change from village to suburb.

The coming of the railway to Woodford also saw the demise of the long distance stage coach but in the latter half of the 19th century and the early 20th century the roads became busier. Not only was the population of Woodford growing larger, but Epping Forest became more and more popular as the 'Cockney Playground'. Trippers, cycle clubs and, later on, motoring clubs saw Woodford as an ideal base to spend a day away from London's smokey environment.

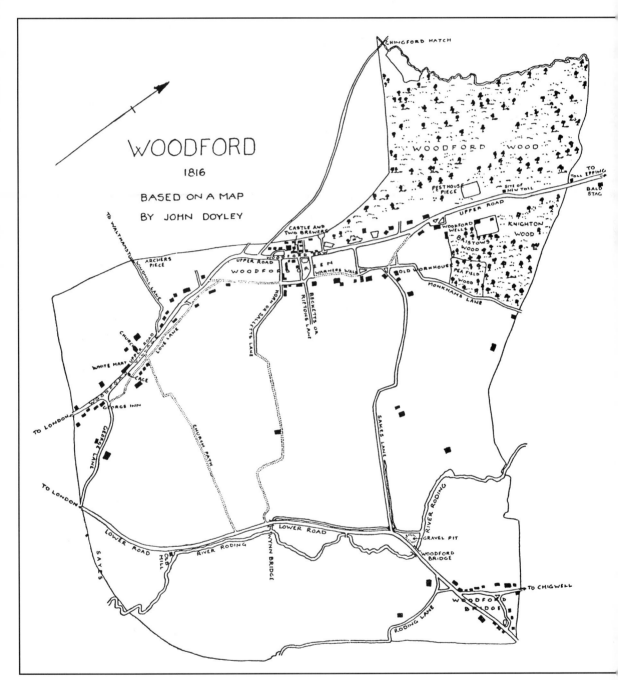

**52** Sketch map of the parish in 1816. This is taken from a very large and detailed map of the land owned by William Pole-Wellesley of Wanstead House, drawn by John Doyley in 1816. The district around the church is called 'Woodford village' while by *The Castle* it is called 'Woodford Row'. The map shows the original course of Sakes or Snakes Lane. This was re-routed (to join up with Becketts Lane) in 1823 when £1,000 was given by Brice Pearse of Monkhams and William Mellish of Harts to build a new workhouse next to the pesthouse (the site now occupied by Bancroft's School).

**53** Aerial view of Woodford Green with Harts to the right. In return for their 'generosity', William Mellish was allowed to extend the western boundary of his property so that the Harts estate now cuts into the Green in a curve. Brice Pearse benefited when the parish moved the course of Snakes Lane to the south. This meant that it no longer passed the front of the house built by Sir John Hall and recently purchased by Brice Pearse. He therefore consolidated all his land holdings into one unit.

**54** The old *White Hart,* Woodford Bridge. This early 19th-century painting used to hang in the nearby *Three Jolly Wheelers* but its present whereabouts is unknown. The stage coach is pulling up outside the inn. The 18th-century cottages opposite were restored in the late 1980s and Roding Lane North can be seen on the left. This ancient access road to Ilford has been known by different names through the centuries: Long Lane in 1403, Rowden Lane in 1517 and Woodford Bridge Road in the 19th century. A section by the P.D.S.A. hospital stills retains that name. The *White Hart* was rebuilt around 1900 (*see* illustration 136).

**55** The Woodford Bridge Toll House, *c.*1860. Built in the 18th century by the Middlesex and Essex Turnpike Trust, it stood on the Chigwell Road where it forks with Manor Road. Also in the view is the turnpike gate and the side of the old *White Hart* inn.

**56** The Woodford Wells Toll House, *c.*1900. The Epping and Ongar Highway Trust opened the turnpike in 1769 and the old toll house seen covered with ivy had to be adapted or moved on two occasions, when the Epping New Road was built in 1834 and again in 1866 when the road from Buckhurst Hill was realigned to make way for an entrance to Knighton mansion. The cottage was taken down in the 1930s but the horse trough was there until the 1960s.

**57** Not strictly of Woodford, this picture shows the old horse pond at the top of Oak Hill, opposite the *Napier Arms*. The bridle path behind the pond was an old cartway which became redundant when the Woodford New Road turnpike was built in 1829, effectively bypassing South Woodford.

**58** Monkhams Lane, *c*.1905. One of the local lanes which were unsurfaced until the 1930s housing boom. Orchard Cottage, now 145 Monkhams Lane, stands alone. It was originally one of the Monkhams estate cottages, now surrounded by 20th-century development.

**59** Woodford Bridge, *c*.1905. Built in 1771, the bridge served until 1962 when it was replaced by a construction more suitable for modern-day traffic needs. The course of the River Roding was changed when the M11 motorway was built.

**60**   *The George, c.*1910. Apart from the traps parked outside the pub, there is a horse bus waiting to move off.

**61**   The *Napier Arms, c.*1914. The Walthamstow district tram service began in 1905 but only as far as the terminus seen here. Woodford district council would not allow the route to extend any further. This decision was repeated when trolley buses were introduced in the 1930s.

**62** Buses outside *The Horse and Well*, *c.*1920. 'Vanguard' buses are shown in the picture. Motor buses first came to Woodford in 1914.

**63** Freeland Grocers delivery van, *c.*1925. F.H. Freeland was a high-class grocer and provision merchant of lower George Lane.

**54** We must assume that the gentleman, photographed in 1926, is a Mr. Wells who ran the 'Express Boot & Shoe Repairing Co' close to where the Woodford Bridge post office is now in the Chigwell Road.

**55** Harvey Hudsons, High Road, South Woodford, *c.*1925. Arthur Steven's haulage lorry, from Whitehall Road, Woodford Wells, is filling up with petrol. The cottage on the left was part of the 18th-century terrace that made way for the Majestic cinema in 1934.

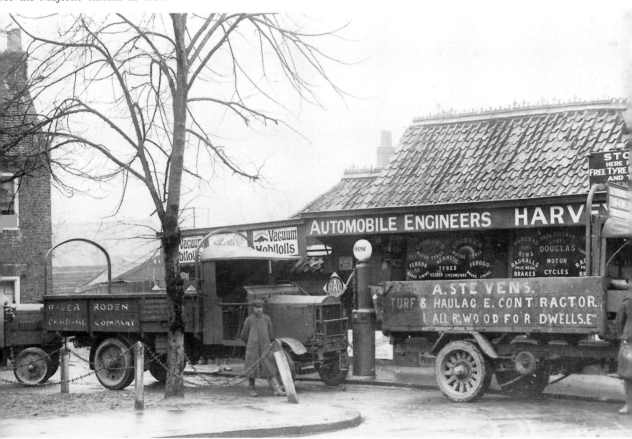

**66** *The Castle*, Woodford Green. By the turn of the century *The Castle* had become one of the favourite places to stop at when visiting the forest. There has been an inn on the site at least since the 1750s but the present building is early 19th-century, with several later alterations.

**67** The Woodford Cycle Meet. This annual event of fun, colour and fund-raising first began in 1882 and, apart from a break in the 1890s, continued until 1914. Cycle clubs were invited to decorate their machines and dress up.

Often businesses sent in representatives. Prizes were given for the best fancy dress, decorated machine, the biggest club muster and the most money raised. It was called the Woodford Cycle Meet as the Green was the assembly place for the judging but the parade started on Wanstead Flats and continued up into Epping Forest. As evening fell, many cyclists would illuminate their machines with chinese lanterns and ride back through Woodford to Wanstead. The money raised went to help orphanages, local and London hospitals. For example, of the £2,980 raised in 1898, the London Hospital received £31 and the Jubilee Hospital, Woodford received £35. A prize giving concert was held at Stratford Town Hall.

**68** 'Summer and Winter', Miss Edith Tibb's entry in the Woodford Cycle Meet, *c*.1911.

**69** 'O-so-silkie', Miss Victoria Hanson's entry in the Woodford Cycle Meet, *c*.1911, advertising crochet cotton.

**70** (*above*) Woodford Railway Crossing, *c*.1918. The Eastern Counties Railway opened a branch line from Stratford to Loughton in 1856. The railway line effectively cut Woodford into two and the social distinction between above and below the line began. By 1860 suburban development had begun. The view in this picture is from Snakes Lane East with the Edwardian Broadway shops in the background.

**71** (*right*) George Lane station, *c*.1918. As with Woodford, a station opened at South Woodford in 1856 and at first it was called George Lane. This picture shows the London-bound platform without the present canopy. This canopy, along with other modifications, was introduced when the Central Line began in 1947. By then the station was known as South Woodford.

**72** (*above right*) George Lane crossing, *c*.1915. Maybank Road is on the right of the picture with the crossing gateman's cottage alongside. In 1897 a letter appeared in the *Woodford Mail* alleging that the reason for the gates being kept shut unnecessarily for 10 minutes was that 'the porter in question was sweethearting around the corner'. The editor commented that a vow of celibacy was required.

# Forest and Enclosures

Epping Forest was preserved as an open space under the guidance and management of the City of London Corporation by the Epping Forest Act of 1878. Apart from a small strip of grassland beside Woodford Road, the forest land in Woodford is at the Green and Woodford Wells. The hedge along Broomhill Road, at the back of the Green, can be dated to about 600 years old and it has obviously served as a boundary between the open grassland and the houses for centuries. However, the extent of the forest at Woodford Wells has changed dramatically in the last 200 years.

The Map of Waltham Forest *c*.1641 shows Woodford Wood, Knighton Wood and Munkom Wood to the north of the parish, but during the 18th century much of Monkham Grove was felled, as this was a legally enclosed, coppiced wood. Woodford Wood remained intact until the 1830s. The Epping and Ongar Highway Trust cut their new road to Epping through the forest in 1830-4, and in 1832 the parish vestry authorised a new road through the forest to Chingford (Whitehall Road). This was built as a means of providing work for local men who might otherwise have been sent to the workhouse. The Overseer of the Poor at that time was Richard Hallett who was also Surveyor of Highways. Once the road had been constructed, houses were soon built beside it on land taken from the forest.

Up until the 19th century the Forest Laws had ensured that land was not enclosed without proper payment to the Crown. Unfortunately, the position of chief officer or Lord Warden of Epping Forest was an hereditary position held by Earl Tylney of Wanstead House. When William Pole-Wellesley took over this rôle, he openly flouted the system and allowed small enclosures. Indeed he was in favour of the complete abolition of the Forest system, which would have enabled him to build on much of his own manorial lands in Wanstead and Woodford without any hindrance. The Crown needed to enforce the Forest Laws to obtain the revenue from enclosures, but with its chief officer only concerned about his own best interests, the system rapidly declined.

Attempts had been made to enclose Knighton Wood as early as 1572, but, although the lord of the manor had been licensed to fence part of the woodland, his action led to riots and the fences were thrown down. In 1826 Thomas Russell sold the freehold estate known as Knighton Wood and the documentation traces previous owners back to 1712. In the early 1830s Richard Hallett purchased the wood and contested the limitations put on him as owner by the Forest Laws. The legal wrangle lasted 12 years and was eventually settled by a compromise. In the early 1850s Hallett built Knighton Villa and, eventually, quite a number of other houses in the vicinity.

In 1863 Knighton Villa was bought by Edward North Buxton who extended the house for his large family. He, along with his brother, Sir Thomas Fowell Buxton of Warlies at Upshire, and their cousin, Andrew Johnston of The Firs at Woodford, were leading members of the Commons Preservation Society. This was formed in 1865 to help in the fight to preserve open spaces like Berkhamsted Common and Hampstead Heath. It was the determination of the members of that society, combined with the might of the City of London Corporation, which eventually led to the saving of Epping Forest. Another influential figure from Woodford Green, Henry Ford Barclay of Monkhams, was also involved as one of the Commissions appointed by the Crown to consider the whole problem and put forward a practical solution.

The vast mass of documentation collected by the Commission provides a wealth of information about the forest in the 1870s. At Woodford Wells most of the wood had been cleared and what had not been covered by houses and gardens was grassland or rough grazing. There was considerable controversy when Diedrich Schwinge of Hanover House (at the junction of the High Road and Whitehall Road) tried to enclose the land in front of his house, much as many of his neighbours were doing. In his case the land was known as 'Roundings Green' and was regarded as part of the village green in front of *The Horse and Well*.

With the passing of the legislation which preserved Epping Forest, all land not actually enclosed as house or garden was purchased by the City of London Corporation and put back into Epping Forest. The ancient Woodford Wood had been destroyed and the forest land here today is largely grassland, scrub or secondary woodland.

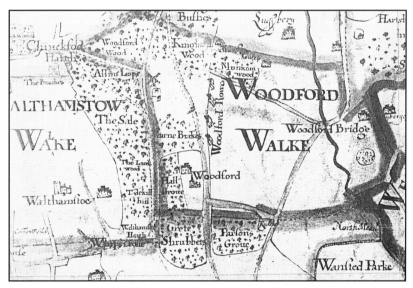

**73** (*above*) Map of the Foresters' Walks in Waltham Forest, *c*.1641. This map was produced to show the area or 'walk' assigned to each keeper. The Master Keepers were usually men of standing in the community (names include William Hunt, Charles Foulis and William Raikes), while the Under Keepers actually carried out the work of ensuring that the Forest Laws were enforced. The map is notoriously inaccurate in some respects but it does give some idea of the extent of the tree cover at that time.

**74** (*left*) The Pulpit Oak, Monkhams Lane. This tree actually stands at the edge of Lords Bushes in Buckhurst Hill, but it has served as a parish boundary marker for several centuries. Perhaps it was called the Pulpit Oak because it was used as such by the preacher when beating the bounds on Rogation Sunday.

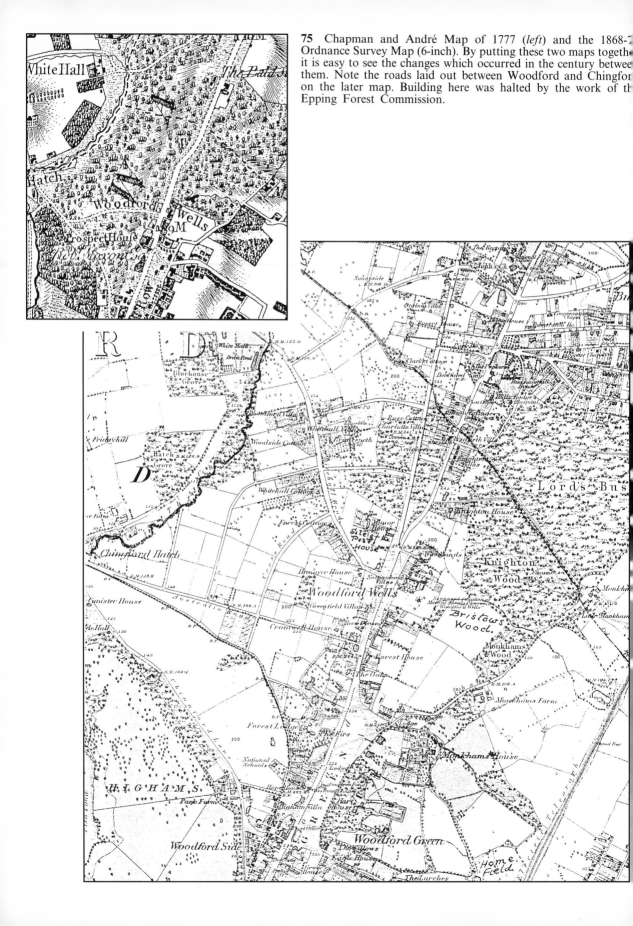

**75** Chapman and André Map of 1777 (*left*) and the 1868-7_ Ordnance Survey Map (6-inch). By putting these two maps togeth__ it is easy to see the changes which occurred in the century betwee_ them. Note the roads laid out between Woodford and Chingfor_ on the later map. Building here was halted by the work of th_ Epping Forest Commission.

6 The Birkbeck Stone on Whitehall Plain. This marker looks very like a milestone, but it stands under a tree to the east of Brook Road. It is inscribed BIRKBECK 1872 and marks a plot owned by the Birkbeck Freehold Land Society who planned to build houses here. They were more successful with a plot taken from Perryman's Farm at Newbury Park, Ilford, and at Leyton, where they owned houses in North Birkbeck and South Birkbeck Roads in the 1870s.

7 155 Whitehall Road. This is one of the oldest houses to have survived beside Whitehall Road. It was probably built in the 1840s on land enclosed by a Mr. Wildman.

**78** Woodford Golf Course. Once the ancient woodland adjacent to Chingford Lane had been cleared, the part near Chingford Hatch was used as arable land, while further up the hill it was grassland. The Epping Forest Act enables land to be set aside from the forest for sport and Woodford Golf Course was created in 1890. Sir J.R. Roberts was president of the club from 1894 until his death in 1917.

**79** The Gipsy Smith Memorial. At the time of the Epping Forest Act gipsies were quite a nuisance in some parts of the forest. However the site of one encampment has become special, as it was under a hornbeam tree near Mill Plain that Gipsy Rodney Smith was born on 31 March 1860. As a child he attended the Methodist Sunday School in Walthamstow and he grew up to become a great evangelist, travelling and preaching right across the world. Gipsy Rodney Smith preached the gospel with love and simplicity and many people were drawn to Christianity through his oratory. He died on 4 August 1947 while on board the *Queen Mary*, on his way to America. On 2 July 1949 a ceremony was held to unveil a rugged boulder of Cornish granite marking the place of his birth. The service was attended by representatives of many religious denominations and hundreds of people joined in, listening to the service from microphones hung in the trees.

**80** (*right*) Edward North Buxton (1840-1924). Descended from Sir Thomas Fowell Buxton, who fought with Wilberforce to abolish slavery, and the famous Quaker family The Gurneys of Earlham, Edward North Buxton was a man of authority, wisdom and kindness. His principal love was for nature and much of his time was spent in helping to preserve open spaces. He was largely responsible for the opening of Hainault Forest as a recreation area and in securing Hatfield Forest for the National Trust. He played a leading rôle in the fight to save Epping Forest and served as a verderer for 44 years. He and his wife Emily lived at Knighton for over 60 years and, though very different in personality, they were a devoted couple (*see also* illustration 152).

**81** (*above*) Knighton, *c.*1900. Built in the early 1850s, the house became the home of Edward and Emily Buxton in 1862, soon after their marriage. Their daughter Theresa described her home as 'a small villa, added to 19 times to meet their increasing family and to take the trophies of Big Game shooting. I think its success as a house was due to my father's original and foreseeing mind as he evolved from the small villa a large house with a big hall and staircase, with the organ half way up, wide gallery, big sitting rooms and bedrooms. It was hideous but what was called commodious. It caught all the sun and was very light.' The house was demolished in 1935.

**82** (*below*) Knighton Lake. Edward North Buxton created the lake on his estate as an amenity for his family who enjoyed swimming, boating and fishing there. When it froze in the winter the banks were lit with chinese lanterns and tar barrels and the local people were invited to come and skate. The gardens were also opened to the public when the fine collection of rhododendrons and azaleas were in bloom. Knighton Wood and the lake were added to Epping Forest in 1930.

# A Time of Change

Although it has been said that the building of the railway started the change from village to suburb, this did not happen immediately, nor quickly. No doubt some additional houses were constructed in the late 1850s, just as they were in the late 1840s, to accommodate the ever-growing population. But the first housing estate to be built was on part of the Woodford Hall parkland, starting with Chelmsford Road in 1867. The British Land Company had purchased the land and sold single and double plots for development. The roads were named after the Earl of Derby's third cabinet, currently in office (Derby, Peel, Walpole, Carnarvon, Stanley, Malmesbury and Buckingham). Woodford Hall itself was used as a convalescent home for up to 80 inmates. Mrs. Gladstone, wife of the Liberal politician, had established a home at Clapton for the poor of London during a cholera epidemic in 1866. This was amalgamated with a similar home established at Snaresbrook and transferred to Woodford Hall in 1869.

In 1870 Maybank, Daisy, Violet, Cowslip and nearby roads were built on the Rookery estate which had been severed by the railway line. The first shop in the parade, known as Orchard House, just below the line, was a 'fancy repository' opened in 1878 by Miss Naomi Pearce. Development of the Grove Hall estate started in 1872 with Grove Hill etc. and by 1876 building near Woodford station was increasing in the Prospect Road area, off lower Snakes Lane.

The ancient ecclesiastical parish had been divided in 1854 when St Paul's Church was built at Woodford Bridge, saving local residents the long walk to St Mary's. C.B. Waller, assistant curate at Woodford, was the first vicar of St Paul's, as it was largely due to his efforts that the money for the new building had been raised. The church was badly damaged by a fire in 1880 and was rebuilt six years later. By this time the parish had been further sub-divided when All Saints' Church was built at Woodford Wells. Henry Ford Barclay had given land for the church at Inmans Row in 1874. A Roman Catholic church was built in 1895 thanks to the generosity of Henrietta Pelham-Clinton, Dowager Duchess of Newcastle. The church, dedicated to St Thomas of Canterbury, is also at Woodford Wells.

In 1882 Woodford could still be described as a large and scattered parish as there were working farms between Snakes Lane and George Lane (Roots and Milkwell Farms) and many large estates still intact. The River Roding was a pretty stream flowing through meadows rich with wild flowers in the summer but likely to flood in winter. At Woodford Wells the open green attracted many visitors and on a Sunday a hundred or more traps would be parked there.

The principal shopping centre in 1882 was at Woodford Green where there were also churches serving several denominations. Various 'institutions' had been established to encourage education among the working classes and these included art and industry, music, horticulture, debating and a 'Young Men's Mutual Improvement Society'. There were post offices at four locations in 1882, with that run by Miss Hoye at Woodford Green boasting 'Letters dispatched at 9.50 am, 12.45, 3.20, 4.45 and 9.30 pm and delivered at 8.15 am, 1.15, 4.30 and 8.30 pm'.

Although there were quite a number of private schools in Woodford, the first school for local children was established in Sunset Avenue in 1814. This has continued, with changes in management, funding and building, right up until the present day. A school was opened at Woodford Bridge in 1859, attached to St Paul's Church, but this had closed by 1906 and the premises now serve as the church halls. A School Board was formed for Woodford in 1871 and, apart from taking over the two schools already mentioned, a new school was opened at Churchfields in 1873. Other schools were built at Cowslip Road in 1897 and at Ray Lodge in 1904. Education in the parish has undergone many changes since then.

House building continued with the development of the Monkhams estate, starting in 1903 and continuing in stages up until the Second World War. Part of the old kitchen garden wall still stands by Twentyman Close and the building known as Norman Court is quite easily recognised as the stable block illustrated in the 1903 sale catalogue. In 1907 Ivy House (near *The Cricketers* on Salway Hill) was demolished and the site built over. The old garden wall is still standing near the end of Empress Avenue. The first council estate was built in 1920 on land on the east side of the railway, near Snakes Lane. Overall, an average of 660 new houses were built each year in the 1920s and this figure rose to 1,600 in the 1930s.

In 1925 the Southend Road was opened, linking Woodford with the extensive area of new housing around Gants Hill. Apparently there was at least one elderly lady who wanted to drive down it in her carriage! This road cut through the Elmhurst estate and opened the way for development of Hill Farm, near Roding Lane. The Laings Estate was begun after Salway House was demolished in 1931. As one by one the old élite of Woodford passed away, the mansions were demolished and Woodford became suburbanised.

Woodford lost its civic identity in 1934 when it joined with Wanstead to become an urban district. As the principal manors had been linked since 1710, this unity was a natural step forward. A municipal borough charter was presented on 14 October 1937 amid great rejoicing, and nobody thought then that within 30 years the new borough would have been swept away as Wanstead and Woodford were joined with Ilford to become the London Borough of Redbridge.

The following illustrations take the reader on a stroll around the parish in the early years of this century. The authors make no apology for following the style of *Woodford then and now* by Reg Fowkes, and recommend those who would like to see more pictures from the same period, coupled with present-days views, to obtain a copy of that book.

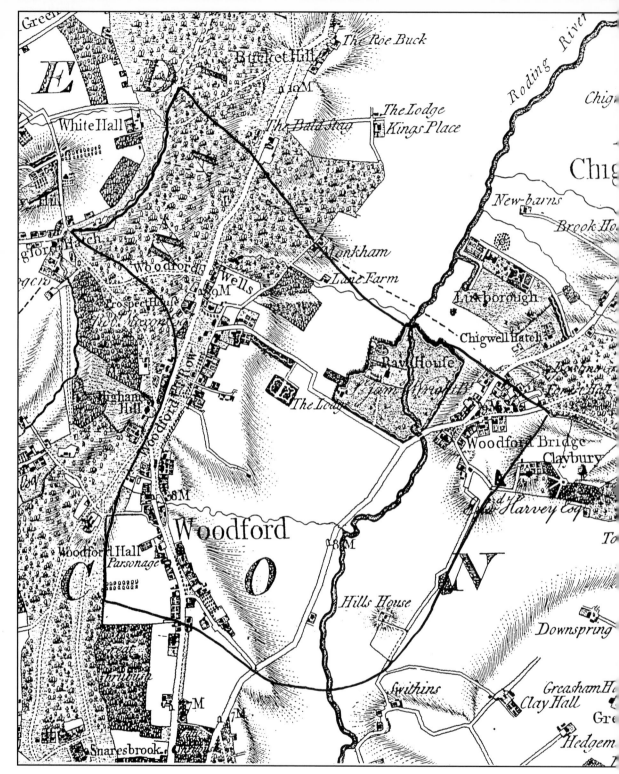

**83** Chapman and André Map, published in 1777. The parish outline (as at 1933) has been drawn onto this version of the map which is an enlargement of the map shown in the first illustration.

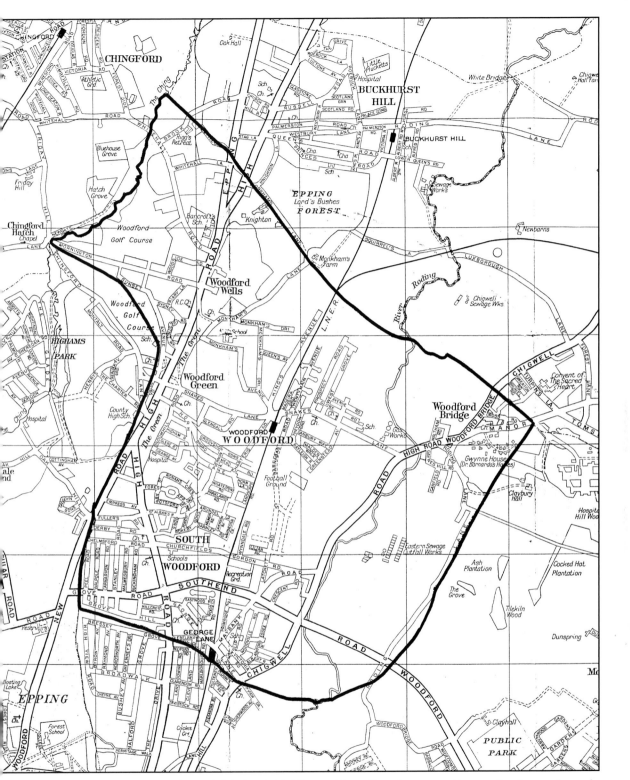

**84** The 'Geographia' London Atlas, published *c.*1933. The parish outline shown on this map has been enhanced so that a comparison can be made with the previous map of the parish, made about 150 years earlier.

85 An illustration from *The Builder*, 26 November 1881, shows a proposed house in Woodford. The house shown is similar to the large house that stands in Broomhill Road by the junction with Fairfield Road. It highlights the fact that fine houses in Woodford were still very much in demand in the late Victorian period.

86 Lower George Lane, *c.*1915. It is hard to imagine that only 70 years before, with no railway, there were just three large houses (The Rookery, Frithmans and Grove Lodge), stables and farm buildings in George Lane. The Market, on the corner of Pulteney Road, was built in the 1880s.

**87** Lower George Lane, *c.*1908. The shops on the right, nearest to the *Railway Bell,* are the oldest shops in George Lane, dating from 1878. Freeland Grocers (*see* illustration 63) is in the centre of the picture.

**88** The *Railway Bell*, George Lane, *c*.1915. Records show that alcohol was officially being sold here from 1878 but the building could a little earlier. The shops in the picture, as mentioned earlier, are the oldest in George Lane. They were known as Orchard House and Orchard Terrace, a reminder of what was there before.

**89** Chigwell Road, South Woodford, *c*.1910, looking towards the Old Mill garage, which was demolished in the 1970s to make way for the enlarged Charlie Brown roundabout. The houses on the right were known as Windsor Terrace and backed onto the River Roding. They were flooded every winter and eventually they were demolished in the 1950s. An open field now marks the site and the river has also gone, diverted when the M11 was built.

**90** Maybank Road, South Woodford, one of a series of roads which included Daisy, Voilet and Cowslip, all laid out in the 1870s. The children are gathered around a newly installed gas lamp at the junction with Violet Road. The gas was supplied by the Chigwell & Woodford Bridge Gas Company in Snakes Lane. The houses on the right were demolished in the 1970s to make way for the motorway.

**91**  Class I, Cowslip Road Board School, *c*.1921. This photograph of an infant class was taken in temporary accommodation in Oakdale Road. The original buildings in Cowslip Road, opened in 1897, were used for the older children by the 1920s.

**92**  Mayday celebrations, *c*.1922. Probably the same class as the previous picture, but a year later, showing the children's Mayday celebrations.

93 George Lane station, *c.*1910. The station house was originally built with two storeys, but by 1912 it had been reduced to the present size. The carriage in the centre of the picture is probably a cab for hire.

94 This parade in George Lane was complete by 1900, although the shops on the right-hand side suffered from bombing during the last war and have been rebuilt. The original occupiers, Edwin Walker, Parr's Bank and Pickerings have gone but Freeman, Hardy & Willis remains as the oldest business name in George Lane.

George Lane, South Woodford.

To be obtained only of Edwin T. Walker Stationer George Lane.

**95** This 1920s view of George Lane shows that the shops extended only as far as Cleveland Road. The tower of what became 'Warnes', the school uniform supplier, can be seen on the left.

**96** Cleveland Road, South Woodford, is one of a block of streets near to George Lane station, with houses built for more wealthy Victorian commuters.

97 George Lane, about 1914. The Congregational church was built in 1886 but was demolished to make way for a frozen food store. The garden on the left has separated George Lane from the Shrubberies since 1900. The drinking fountain was unveiled by Miss Emma Fowler of Glebelands in 1899.

98 This group of buildings in the High Road, opposite Grove Hill, although completely restored, dates back to the 1750s with additions in the 19th century. For two hundred years, Liddle's the grocers served the people of Woodford. They correctly boasted in a 1950s advert that they were the oldest grocers in Essex.

**99** High Road, South Woodford, *c*.1905. This picture shows the view from the junction with George Lane, looking south. The cottages beyond *The George* were demolished in the early 1930s and the cinema now occupies the site.

**100** High Road, South Woodford in the 1920s. This view is looking north along the footway opposite the top of George Lane. The policeman is standing by the wooden police telephone box which was placed on ground belonging to the Grove. The ground rent was one shilling (5p) per year. The Grove was demolished after the last war and the Fenchurch Insurance offices now occupy the site.

**101** Elmhurst Gardens, South Woodford, *c.*1930. The gardens were opened in July 1927 as the Woodford Recreation Ground on land purchased by Woodford Urban District Council in 1921 from Mr. Lister Harrison of Elmhurst. The house is now part of the Queen Mary College halls of residence. The ground used for Elmhurst Gardens was separated from the rest of the estate by the railway line in 1856.

**102** Haymaking in the Rectory Field, *c.*1900. This picture comes from an album compiled in 1904 while Rev. Albert Hughes was the Rector. It is captioned 'Cousin Angela with her friend'.

**103** St Mary's Church, *c.*1920. The nanny pushing a pram must have been a common sight in Woodford in the earlier years of this century.

**104** Radbourne's Dairy, *c.*1910. The dairy was situated at 22 High Road, selling milk from farms at Harlow, Walthamstow and from Churchfields Farm, opposite. Their delivery men did three rounds a day, pushing a handcart with a three-gallon churn, starting at 5a.m. and finishing at 4p.m. Customers were served using the imperial measures which were hanging on the cart. In those days milk was 2d. a pint (less than one new pence) and the men earned 18s. (90p) a week.

**105**  Gladstone Terrace, High Road, *c.*1914. This Victorian parade of shops stands at the junction with Derby Road, on part of the site previously occupied by stabling and farm buildings belonging to Woodford Hall. The premier house in Woodford stood where the back section of the Memorial Hall is today.

**06**  Wooden cottages on alway Hill, *c.*1930. There were number of weather-boarded hops and cottages like these long the west side of the High Road at South Woodford in he early years of this century. he cottages shown were north f the junction with Derby Road and were demolished in 935.

**107**  Salway Hill, pictured just after the First World War. *The Cricketers* pub is in the foreground, with the clock tower of the stable block of Pyrmont, now a day nursery, visible over the chimneys of the adjacent cottages. The road takes its name from Richard Salway (*c.*1701-75), a Turkey merchant and Director of the Bank of England, who lived at Salway Lodge, on the opposite side of the road, in the 18th century.

**108**  The Willows, Offices of Woodford Urban District Council. The Official Guide Book for 1924 says: 'The seat of government for Woodford is located in an old mansion standing in its own grounds at the corner of Snakes Lane, and looking away over the western end of Woodford Green. The Clerk's Office and that of the Rate Collector are on the first floor, the Surveyor's is on the ground floor, and the Sanitary Inspector is located in the basement. The

Council Chamber, evidently the dining room of the mansion, is a long apartment on the ground floor with a pleasant garden outlook in the rear. It contains a handsome marble mantelpiece. On the walls hang a number of portraits of notable members and chairmen of the Council. There is also a framed copy of the Address presented by Woodford and five other parishes to King George and Queen Mary on the occasion of their visit to open the Chingford Reservoir of the Metropolitan Water Board, March 15th, 1915, with the Royal reply in typescript by its side. Another mural decoration is the framed Certificate of the Dewar Trophy (founded by Sir Thomas R. Dewar) held by the Woodford Fire Brigade for the year 1906.'

**109** Woodford fire brigade, *c.*1925. From a volunteer force begun in the 1880s, Woodford's fire service developed after the formation of the urban district council in 1894. The station house shown was in the front garden of the Willows, a detached house at the top of Snakes Lane which was used as council offices. The house was demolished in the 1930s to make way for the telephone exchange and the old station house is incorporated into the present fire station complex.

**110** Woodford Green post office, 1905. This postcard commemorates the opening of the building situated in Johnston Road.

**111**  Horn Lane as seen here, *c.*1903, is totally unrecognisable. Originally it was just a track leading from Broomhill Road down to Roots and Milkwell Farms. Roots Farm cottages can be seen on the left with the older properties in Shenfield Road in the distance.

**112**  A post-Second World War view of cricket on Woodford Green, with the ruined Congregational church in the background. Hit twice by rockets in 1944, the site was eventually cleared for the building of the Sir James Hawkey Hall.

**113** Jubilee Hospital, 1926. The local cottage hospital was built with money donated by Sir John Roberts to celebrate the Diamond Jubilee of Queen Victoria's reign. It was opened by the Duke and Duchess of Connaught in 1899, but closed in 1985 and has since been demolished.

**114** The *Wilfrid Lawson Temperance Hotel*, 1907. Andrew Johnston and his wife were champions of the temperance cause and established the hotel as a social centre for Woodford and to cater for visitors to Epping Forest. It opened in 1883, but was demolished in 1974 after having been used for some time as a nurses' training centre.

**15** *The Castle* has been a dominant building on Woodford Green for over two centuries. Like many other local pubs, by the 1920s it had geared itself to accommodate trippers coming out for a day in Epping Forest.

**16** *The Castle* and Lanehurst, *c.*1910. Behind the pub sign can be seen Lanehurst, a timber-framed house that had a brick façade built onto it during the Georgian period.

**117** High Road, Woodford Green, *c*.1910. This was Woodford's first shopping centre; the section between *The Castle* and the ponds was called High Street. This picture shows the forward encroachment of buildings beyond Mill Lane.

**118** Another view of the shops on Woodford Green. This group of buildings is still complete. Notice the nanny pushing the pram. The Woodford Men's Club (at the edge of the picture) was opened in 1904, using a building that was previously a Union church.

**119** Stephens' china and gift shop, High Road, Woodford Green, photographed about 1924, just before it was modernised. The *Woodford Times* offices on the left remained there until the 1960s when the newspaper was taken over by the *Express & Independent*.

**120 & 121** (*below and opposite right*) Stephens' china and hardware shop, on Woodford Green in 1925, after refurbishment. The business was started in 1881 and the shop sign was Alfred Duggan Stephens' signature.

**122** The Union church at Woodford Green, in 1904. A year later it was converted to the Woodford Men's Club by the generosity of Sir J.R. Roberts. One of the alterations was replacing the spire with a small dome.

**123** The potato pond at Woodford Green. This early photograph is taken from a glass slide, now a little deteriorated. It shows the pump which used to stand by the pond. It is said that local people washed potatoes grown on the land now covered by Woodford Golf Course under the pump during the Irish Potato Famine. The Congregational church can be seen in the background.

**24** This 1930s picture shows The Terrace and the narrow road which led down to Horn Lane. Whilst the Congregational church, after being bombed, was replaced by the Sir James Hawkey Hall, Horn Lane was partly demolished to make way for Broadmead Road after the last war.

**25** All Saints' Church, Inmans Row, was built in 1874 on a site facing the Green, given by Henry Ford Barclay of Monkhams. In 1876 a north aisle was added and in 1885 a choir vestry. The cottages seen have been replaced by larger houses.

**126** Telegraph poles were erected alon[g] the High Road in 1903. Their appearanc[e] cause just as much anger as the coming [of] cable television and communications ha[s] done in the 1990s. The message with thi[s] picture says 'caught in the act of deliberatel[y] and needlessly spoiling much of Woodford['s] picturesqueness'. A similar photograph ha[s] a rhyme with it:

O slender supporter of wire and of copper
Men with ladders are rearing you high in the air,
Will you kindly please fall on their bodies-a
   cropper
For their action has caused forest lovers to swear.

**127** *The Horse and Well*, 1914. Already i[n] existence in 1722, the pub has been a popula[r] venue ever since. Originally this was becaus[e] of the 'mineral springs' and in the earl[y] 1800s the landlord, Tom Rounding, helpe[d] to organise the Epping Hunt. Later, th[e] proximity to Epping Forest was a[n] attraction.

**128**  Monkhams, aerial view, *c.1922.* Monkhams achieved the peak of its grandeur just before 1900 when the owner, Arnold Hills, installed ornamental fountains and other embellishments in the grounds. Financial difficulties led to the sale of the estate to James Twentyman in 1903. During the First World War the mansion was used to house Belgian refugees and at the time of this photograph it was used as a school. It was finally demolished in 1930.

**129**  Monkhams Avenue during the 1920s. When James Twentyman purchased the Monkhams estate he sold off some of the land for housing. Roads were laid out and gradually building started on some of the houses, although the development was not completed until after the death of Mr. Twentyman in 1928.

**130** The Edwardian sweep of the Broadway shops in Snakes Lane is built over a large lake that was part of the Monkhams estate. By 1904 sections of the estate were being developed and these were the first shops erected 'above' the railway line.

**131** The Broadway shops and railway crossing about 1920. At this time, as can be seen by the trees in the background, there was little development 'below' the railway line until you got to Claremont Grove.

**132** Woodford station, *c.*1910. Like the station house at George Lane, that at Woodford was also built with two storeys and the original building is unaltered. In the early 1990s the ticket office was given a major facelift and a single-storey waiting area was added at the front.

**133** Snakes Lane East, with the dairy buildings of Glengall Farm partly hiding St Barnabas' Church, which was completed in 1911 and extended in 1964. This 1920s photograph shows the shops up to and beyond Prospect Road, much as it is today.

**134** Snakes Lane East, just past Prospect Road, *c*.1910. The buildings on the left (known as Alma Terrace) and the streets behind are some of the earliest suburban development in Woodford, having been laid out in the 1860s. Alma Terrace is now all shops. On the right can be seen the hedges and buildings of Glengall Farm.

**135** This section of Chigwell Road was known as Pump Hill, as two pumps were placed by the roadside, one either side of the bridge over the Roding. During the building of the motorway in the 1970s, the surviving pump that stood opposite the end of Snakes Lane was rescued and is now in the garden of Wanstead House Community Centre. Some of the Edwardian houses shown in the picture were converted to shops as the population increased.

**136** The present *White Hart* at Woodford Bridge, as seen in this 1920s view, was rebuilt about 1900 on the site of an 18th-century inn. Roding Lane North, on the left, was previously known as Woodford Bridge Road and is the old route to and from Ilford before the Woodford Avenue was built in the 1920s. Note the open fields of central Woodford in the distance.

**137** Several of these mid-19th-century buildings in Woodford Bridge were originally farm labourers' cottages. By 1910 this road was known as High Road, Woodford Bridge. The site of the Middlesex and Essex turnpike cottage (*see* illustration 55) was at the point where Manor Road joins the High Road.

**138** A charming late 1920s study of the post office at Woodford Bridge. The number 70 on the cottage next door, yet to be converted to a shop, refers to the time when this part of Chigwell Road was the High Road.

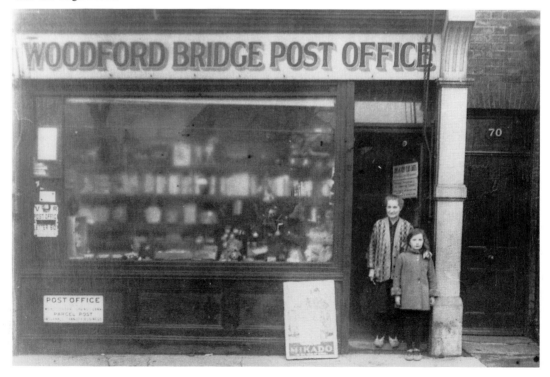

**139** This timeless picture of St Paul's Church, Woodford Bridge, also shows the old fixed gas holder in the Snakes Lane depot. That Woodford landmark was demolished in 1985. The building of St Paul's in 1854 was the first subdivision of the ancient Woodford parish. The church was rebuilt in 1886 after being gutted by fire.

**140** Only five years after St Paul's was built, the wealthy and resourceful vicar, C.B. Waller, organised the building of the church school next door. In this picture, taken about 1910, the schoolmaster's house can be seen, built to a basic design suggested by Prince Albert and seen at the Great Exhibition of 1851.

**141** St Paul's Church School, *c.*1890. The school was opened in 1859 to serve the children of Woodford Bridge, but it had closed by 1906. A banner proclaiming 'Woodford School Board' is on display in this photograph.

**142** By the Upper Green at Woodford Bridge, *c.*1925. The *Crown and Crooked Billet* is the only building still standing today as blocks of flats now border the road here. Note the track across the middle of the Green and extensive gravel diggings, now all flattened and grassed over.

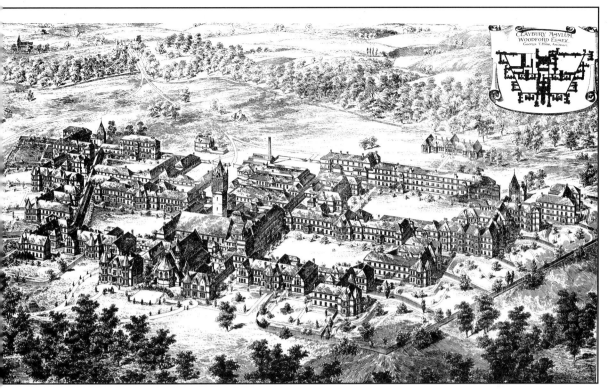

**143** A 'bird's eye' view of the proposed Claybury Hospital complex as published in *The Builder*, 23 November 1889. As well as the arrival of the railway to Woodford in 1856, the building of 'Claybury Asylum' and its opening in 1893 must have had an enormous social and economic impact on the whole area. The Claybury estate, which dates from the medieval period, has always been strictly speaking in the parish of Barking and later Ilford. However, when the estate was purchased in 1887 for £36,000, the 'asylum' buildings were designed to be served by a new main entrance in Manor Road, Woodford Bridge. This entrance, with its lodges, was completed in 1899 and by this time, because of demand, the number of places for patients had risen from 2,005 to 2,500. The statistics of the buildings are staggering and include the fact that the main buildings cover 20 acres and are constructed with 27,000,000 bricks. The late 18th-century Claybury Hall, part of the parkland landscape, and the ancient medieval woodland are still retained within the present hospital grounds.

**144** A view of the hospital administration offices and the water tower, which is such a well known landmark.

## Some More Recent Woodford Worthies

As time went by the railway and the development of housing made Woodford a less desirable place for the wealthy, who could now travel further afield more easily and could sell their estates for building land at a good profit. But this was a gradual process and in the 1850s Woodford was still relatively rural. When Henry Fowler and his wife decided to move to Glebelands at the southern end of Woodford in 1852, relatives at Knotts Green, Leyton, were concerned for their safety, living so close to Epping Forest. He was a tea dealer from Wiltshire and had married Ann Ford Barclay (sister of Joseph Gurney Barclay, the banker) in 1848. They were both committed Quakers, and in 1856 Henry Fowler was deprived of four lambs valued at £4 as he refused to pay his church rates. They had 10 children who all did them great credit. Their eldest son, J.Gurney Fowler, became a senior partner in the firm of Price, Waterhouse & Co., Chartered Accountants, as well as serving as a local councillor.

There was a significant cluster of Quaker families living at Plaistow in the 1840s but, as time went by, some married outside The Friends and came to settle further away. Ann Fowler's cousin, Henry Ford Barclay, came to Monkhams in 1864. By then Elizabeth Fry's eldest son, John Gurney Fry, was living at Hale End House by the River Ching (at Highams Park) and his brother Joseph lived near *The George* at Wanstead. In 1866 Elmhurst (now part of Queen Mary College halls of residence in the High Road) became the home of Smith Harrison and his wife Jane, sister of Lord Lister, another deeply committed Quaker couple. Like Henry Fowler, Smith Harrison was a tea merchant and a much respected member of Woodford's community. His son, A. Lister Harrison, also took an active part in public life until he moved away from the district.

By 1870 Woodford Hall was being used as a convalescence home but Highams was still a family home, having been purchased by Edward Warner in 1849. His son, Sir Thomas Courtenay Warner, was a Liberal M.P. who entertained Mr. Gladstone at Highams. The family, as lords of the manor of Higham Bensted, built the 'Warner estates' over much of their land in Walthamstow and in 1891 sold 30 acres of the Highams parkland (including the lake) to the City of London Corporation, to be added into Epping Forest. The family left the district in 1902 and the house was leased out. It is now part of Woodford County High School for Girls.

As the most prestigious citizens passed away or left the district, the population was gradually changing, with an increase in the middle classes. Many detached houses were built, attracting those who were comfortably off, and who employed two or three maids, rather than an army of servants. It was accepted in late Victorian and Edwardian times that most young girls would go into service. Their wages were low and they were expected to work long hours, but they were fed, clothed and warm, and many had a good relationship with their employers.

There are still a few elderly residents of Woodford who can remember having a nanny and going to bed by candlelight; the doctor coming in a pony-trap, and the grocer's boy delivering on a bicycle; the lamplighter, and the smell of the earth when the water-cart came round to settle the dust on the un-made roads in the summer. A number of the wealthiest Woodfordians would invite the local (upper class) children for a party at Christmas. There were 'At Home' afternoon teas, and garden parties in the summer.

There was also poverty in Woodford, but that was kept 'below the line'. The railway created a social divide in more ways than one. The big houses had always been along the High Road at Woodford Row and the first council houses were built off Snakes Lane, east of the railway. There was some industry here too, as the quantity of new houses being built made a ready demand for bricks. As there was a good supply of natural brickearth in the Roding valley, several brickworks were established near the river by W.& C. French, Gales and Barretts.

In 1909 a new chapter in the history of Woodford started with the opening of Dr. Barnardo's Garden City Home for Boys at Woodford Bridge. The first stage in the project was the purchase of Gwynne House (now *The Prince Regent Hotel*) and adjoining land. The plan was to build 30 detached houses for the boys to live in, under the supervision of a house-mother, and this gradually became a reality. Dr. Barnardo had died in 1905 but he had started the Girls Village Home at Barkingside in 1876, and this site still houses the headquarters of the organisation today. The expansion for boys was a natural progression and by 1930 the 'City' at Woodford Bridge provided for 700 boys with a chapel, a hospital, and training facilities for the boys, such as a bakery. The community flourished throughout the 1930s and Woodford Bridge was proud to boast the first Barnardo's boy to gain a degree at London University.

After the First World War, times changed for Woodford residents, just as else-where. The need for women to work while their men were away fighting had opened a door of opportunties which would never be closed, while the invention of modern conveniences made domestic servants redundant. In 1927 the Rector, Rev. William Albery, tired of trying to find domestic staff for the large Georgian rectory by St Mary's Church, moved into the *Wilfrid Lawson Hotel*. The rectory was later sold to the newly formed Wanstead and Woodford Urban District Council, to be used as council offices.

Our story draws to a close with the grant of the Municipal Borough Charter to Wanstead and Woodford on 14 October 1937. The Duke of Gloucester presented the Charter of Incorporation at the Council Offices (previously the rectory) and among the dignitaries present were the Mayor, James Hawkey, and the local M.P., Winston Churchill. The suburbanisation of Woodford was now complete.

**145** Sir John Reynolds Roberts, Bt. (1835-1917). J.R. Roberts was one of several wealthy gentlemen living in Woodford during the late Victorian period whose generosity was seen through the institutions they founded. He provided funds to complete the Jubilee Hospital (1899), the Memorial Hall (1902) and the Woodford Men's Club (1904). His wealth came from the large department store he owned in Stratford Broadway. He lived in Salway House until he died in 1917.

**146** Salway House. This house stood at the top of Salway Hill, next to Hurst House and Salway Lodge, the home of the Salway family in the 18th century. It was originally a farm house but J.R. Roberts bought the house in 1880 and greatly enlarged it. Salway Hall Evangelical church now occupies the site.

**147** The Duchess of Marlborough opens extensions to the Jubilee Hospital in 1911. Also on the platform can be seen several prominent local citizens: (left to right) Mr. J. Gurney Fowler, Dr. Percy Warner, the Duchess of Marlborough, Rev. Canon Sanders (Rector of Woodford), Sir John Roberts and Mr. W.H. Brown.

**148** Glebelands, *c.*1905. This house stood close to the parish boundary with Wanstead and was fairly small when Henry and Ann Fowler arrived in 1852. The arrival of their increasing family necessitated the addition of more bedrooms, accommodation for servants and such. The garden had an assortment of outbuildings and greenhouses. Although the house was demolished in 1915, a stable block still survives in Glebelands Avenue, now used as a nursing home.

**149** Henry Ford Barclay (1826-91)
H.F. Barclay was a descendant of one
of England's oldest Quaker families
which founded the bank of that name.
Henry married Richenda Gurney,
daughter of Samuel Gurney of West
Ham, and they moved to Monkhams
in 1864. He was Chairman of the
Becontree Bench of Magistrates and
served as one of the Epping Forest
Commissioners in the 1870s. Henry
Ford Barclay gave the land so that All
Saints' Church could be built in Inmans
Row. He was a cousin of Ann Ford
Fowler of Glebelands, South Woodford,
and uncle of Edward North Buxton of
Knighton.

**150** Monkhams, 1903. The name is a very ancient one and was given to an earlier house before Brice Pearse purchased this building and demolished the older house. He built up an extensive estate in the early 1800s and there are several later estate cottages still surviving in the area. During the time of Henry Ford Barclay it was said of Monkhams that 'It would be difficult to find a home where old-fashioned English family life was more perfectly exemplified'.

**51**  A society wedding at St Mary's Church. It is very likely that this was the marriage of Henry Ford Barclay's eldest daughter, Edith, to Mr. Francis Maltby Bland, Esq. of Wanstead in July 1872.

To quote from a newspaper report of the time:

'Never perhaps in the history of Woodford was there witnessed such a brilliant assemblage of persons and such general rejoicing as was to be seen on Friday last, the occasion of Miss Barclay's marriage. From one end of the parish to the other the most lively interest was exhibited in the event; tradesmen closed their shops, decorated the fronts of their houses with flags, garlands, wreaths, flowers, mottoes, and devices, and determined to share in the general holiday ... The excitement became intense as score after score of carriages drove up to the church gates and deposited their freight of beauty and fashion ... the friends and relations of the bride who occupied the centre of the church, all elegantly dressed in silks and satins of every shade of colour from the delicate peach to the deepest violet, made in the latest fashion, and most of them trimmed with costly lace, formed a most brilliant spectacle.' The guest list included a host of Barclays, Gurneys, Buxtons, Frys and Chapmans, Mr. & Mrs. Henry Fowler, Mr. & Mrs. Andrew Johnston, Mr. & Mrs. Vigne ...

'The bride, attired in a white satin dress, cut square, trimmed en train with a broad flounce of Brussells lace, tulle and satin trimming round the edge of the skirt; white tulle veil, and a wreath of orange flower, myrtle, and jessamine round her head, was holding a magnificent bouquet, the gift of Mrs. Gladstone, wife of the Premier.' There were 12 bridesmaids and 14 young lady attendants. The ceremony was performed by the Ven. George Bland, Archdeacon of Durham, uncle to the groom.

'The wedding breakfast for nearly 200 guests was given at Monkhams. During the afternoon and evening the mansion and grounds were thrown open to the public and many hundreds took the opportunity of viewing the wedding presents and seeing the estate. Later in the evening a grand display of fireworks, manufactured by Mr. Brock of Crystal Palace, took place in Mr. E.N. Buxton's field, opposite Monkhams Farm, where thousands of spectators from neighbouring parishes were present. At 10 o'clock a grand ball was given at Knighton, in honour of the occasion.

'Considerable activity was given to the trade of the parish by the wedding: drapers and dressmakers were very busy. Mr. Bottle supplied the druggetting for the church, and through him the order was given for the decoration and illumination of the carriage drive. Mrs. Cricks had the honour of making the bonnets for the bridesmaids, and the Dolly Varden hats for the juvenile attendants; she also supplied and trimmed the hats for the school children. The aprons and cross-overs were also made in the parish; and in many other ways the trade received an impetus.'

**152** Mr. and Mrs. Edward North Buxton in 1922. This gentleman has already been mentioned in connection with the fight to save Epping Forest (*see* illustration 80). He was the chairman of the Truman Hanbury Buxton brewery, Justice of the Peace, Deputy Lieutenant for Essex and High Sheriff in 1888, and served for a short time as a Member of Parliament. He married Emily Digby, who was descended from Lord Coke of Holkham Hall in Norfolk, and this picture was taken on the steps of Knighton on the occasion of their diamond wedding anniversary.

**153** The visit of the Prince of Wales to Knighton 23 June 1883. E.N. Buxton was chairman of the London Schools Board and the Prince and Princess of Wales visited Knighton with a distinguished company to see a demonstration of Swedish Drill (physical exercises) by the school children. Mr. Buxton had become acquainted with the Prince during foreign travels. He also came to know Theodore Roosevelt, President of the United States, who stayed at least one night at Knighton when he came to England in May 1910 for the funeral of King Edward VII.

**54** Andrew Johnston (1835-1922). Mr. Johnston lived a large part of his life at the Firs, on Woodford Green, the site now developed as Firs Walk. He was liberal M.P. for South Essex from 1868 to 1874. He served as Chairman of Essex Quarter Sessions, High Sheriff of Essex and Chairman of the local magistrates. With his Buxton cousins he was also involved in the fight to save Epping Forest, and was named as a verderer in the 1878 Epping Forest Act. He was the first chairman of Essex County Council, and served in that rôle for 22 years. He married Charlotte Trevelyan in 1858 and on the occasion of their Golden Wedding the sum of £1,000, raised by friends, was given for the provision of a large swimming bath at Dr. Barnardo's Boys' Home at Woodford Bridge.

**55** The Firs, Woodford Green. Probably built around 1804, the house was the home of Richard Dowding, a cooper from Wapping, certainly from 1815 for at least 30 years. Andrew Johnston lived at the Firs in the second part of the century but had moved next door to Forest Lodge by 1898. Henry Cook then occupied The Firs.

**156** Gwynne House, Woodford Bridge. Gwynne House was built in 1816 by Henry Burmester, a wealthy merchant whose table tomb is found at the front of St Mary's churchyard in the High Road. In 1909 the house and adjoining land was purchased by the Council of Dr. Barnardo's Homes and the 'Garden City Home for Boys' was opened.

**157** 'Saturday House', Barnardo's Boys Garden City. By 1920, 16 of these houses were built, each to provide accommodation for 30 boys, in two dormitories of fifteen. Each house was supervised by a House-mother or Matron. By 1931 there were 34 such houses.

**158** The Chapel of the Good Shepherd, Barnardo's Boys Garden City. There were 700 boys in the Garden City by 1930 and the Chapel was opened and dedicated by the Bishop of Chelmsford in October of that year.

**159** Dr. Barnardo's Garden City. Another view of the boys' 'Houses'. The Garden City was also equipped to teach the boys trades such as baking, tailoring, bootmaking and gardening. Although the 'Boyland Township' began as an experiment, it served a need until closure in September 1977.

**160** The Right Rev. Edgar Jacob, DD, Bishop of St Albans. Dr. Jacob was the son of the Archdeacon and Canon of Winchester and after leaving Oxford University embarked on a distinguished career in the church. He was appointed Bishop of St Albans in 1903 and lived at Highams for a time, with his sister as housekeeper.

**161** Woodford County High for Girls One of Woodford Green's mos impressive buildings stands in fact in Walthamstow. The house, known a Highams, was built in 1768 for the Lore of the Manor of Walthamstow, Anthony Bacon, M.P., to the designs of William Newton (*see* illustration 36). The Warne family, known for their housing estate in Walthamstow, owned the house from 1849. During the First World War the house was used as a military hospital then in 1919 Essex County Council rente the house and grounds and Woodford County High was opened in the September. The County Council late bought the property for £7,000.

**162** Woodford County High School pupils in the early 1920s. When the school first opened in 1919, 110 girls arrived an the 30 who wanted to stay to dinner ha this meal cooked by the nearby *Wilfri Lawson Temperance Hotel*. There was n school dining room until 1927.

**163** The Oaks, *c.*1930. Built in the 18th century, this was the home of the Vigne family for over sixty years. Godfrey Vigne (1801-63) travelled extensively, visiting North and South America, and India. The books he wrote about his journeys gave a valuable insight for his contemporaries. His brother Henry stayed at home and was Master of a pack of harriers used for hare-hunting. Towards the end of the century The Oaks was occupied by the Dowager Duchess of Newcastle. In 1920 the house became a convent but it was demolished in 1974 after a fire and there is now a residential estate on the site.

**164** Henrietta Pelham-Clinton, Dowager Duchess of Newcastle (1843-1913). Henrietta had outlived two husbands before she came to own The Oaks. Her first husband, the 6th Duke of Newcastle, died in 1879 at the age of 45, and she was bereaved again in 1892. The daughter of a wealthy family, Henrietta led a fashionable life in London society, but helped many charitable causes. She purchased The Oaks after the death of Henry Vigne in 1894 and built the Roman Catholic Church of St Thomas of Canterbury, and the adjoining Franciscan friary in the grounds, at her own expense.

**165** Sylvia Pankhurst (1882-1960). Sylvia Pankhurst is best known as a Suffragette, but she spent far more of her life writing and working for peace. After several years fighting for women's rights in the East End, Sylvia moved to Woodford Green and in 1924 she opened a tearoom at the Red Cottage, opposite the *Horse and Well*. Her last 25 years in England were spent at West Dene in Charteris Road. The photograph shows her dictating an anti-Fascist article in her study at West Dene, *c*.1935.

**166** Harts House in 1919. This was probably the third house on the site and was built in 1815 by its owner, William Mellish (*see* illustration 41). The estate was sold in 1919 to East Ham Council and converted into a tuberculosis sanatorium. Many alterations were made and in 1939 a new east wing was built. This wing has been demolished (1995) to make way for a new extension and a new beginning in the long life of this old house and grounds.

**167** Harts House, 'Garden Front'.

**168** William Henry Brown (1845-1918). The photograph shows a Garden Party at Harts *c*.1903 held to commemorate the centenary of the Sunday School Union. Mr. Brown was born in 1845 in Wiltshire, and was a banker and a director of the Metropolitan District Railway. After his retirement he came to live at Harts in 1893 and was the last private occupant of the house. He was a leading liberal and hosted a rally at Harts attended by the Prime Minister in 1905. As chairman of the London Congregational Union he cemented the strength of the nonconformist churches in Woodford. He worshipped at the huge Congregational church that used to stand where the Sir James Hawkey Hall is now. Much of the cost of building that church in 1874 was borne by his predecessor at Harts, Mr. James Spicer. Mr. Brown laid out the water garden at Harts which, we believe, will be retained after the housing development at Harts is complete.

Mr. W. H. Brown.     Mr. Harvey Cook.     Sir H. Campbell-Bannerman.
Mr. A. H. Tozer.     Sir John Roberts.     Mr. Andrew Johnston.

**169** Woodford Worthies 1905. This press photograph from the *Woodford Times* shows a gathering of some of Woodford's most powerful men at a liberal rally in the grounds of Hart's House to hear a speech by the Prime Minister, Sir H. Campbell-Bannerman. Not only were they active in the new politics of the period but they were active in promoting temperance and regular church attendance of all denominations.

**170** 17 Monkhams Avenue. This house in Monkhams Avenue, near to the shops in the Broadway, has a blue plaque which states that Clement Atlee, the post-war labour party Prime Minister and M.P. for Walthamstow, lived there. An elderly lady recalls that 'We lived at 17 Monkhams Lane, but Atlee lived at 17 Monkhams Avenue, and sometimes his laundered shirts were delivered to our house by mistake. My sister and I would take them round and once he came to our house to thank us'.

*Portrait by Cecil Beaton*

## "WE WILL FINISH THE JOB"

"We shall not fail or falter; we shall not weaken or tire. Neither the sudden shock of battle, nor the long-drawn trials of vigilance and exertion will wear us down.

GIVE US THE TOOLS AND WE WILL FINISH THE JOB."

*Mr Churchill's reply to Mr Roosevelt*

**171** Sir Winston Churchill (1874-1965). Churchill represented Woodford from 1924 until 1964 but in the early years Woodford was just part of a much larger constituency of 'Epping Division in Essex'. Eventually as populations increased parliamentary contituencies were subdivided until the Wanstead and Woodford constituency was formed. This famous picture was taken in the cabinet room at 10 Downing Street during the last war.

**172** 14 October 1937 Wanstead and Woodford become a Municipal Borough and among the dignitaries waiting for the Duke of Gloucester are Mayor James Hawkey, Lord Lieutenant Col. F. Whitmore and local M.P. Winston Churchill.

**173** The Duke of Gloucester is greeted by the Lord Lieutenant. His aide is bearing the Charter of Incorporation.

**174** Wartime in George Lane. The damage shown to the shops is the aftermath of two high explosive bombs being dropped on 14 October 1940. Two people were trapped. Author Peter Lawrence says, 'The lorry on the right belonged to my grandfather and the bewildered young lady standing next to it is my aunt who has had her first-floor ladies' hairdressing salon destroyed and is salvaging her belongings.'

**175** A Victorious Prime Minister. A photograph from the *Woodford Times* of 27 May 1945 shows Winston Churchill and his wife replying to the welcoming crowd on Woodford Green, three weeks after V.E. day.